MAKING READING RELEVANT

RELEVANT

THE ART OF CONNECTING

Fourth Edition

MAKING READING RELEVANT

RELEVANT

THE ART OF CONNECTING

Teri Quick
Melissa Zimmer
Diane Hocevar
Metropolitan Community College
Omaha, Nebraska

 **Pearson**

330 Hudson Street, NY, NY 10013

VP & Portfolio Manager: Eric Stano
Development Editor: Katharine Glynn
Marketing Manager: Nick Bolte
Program Manager: Rachel Harbour
Project Manager: iEnergizer Aptara®, Ltd.
Cover Designer: Pentagram
Cover Illustration: freshidea/Fotolia
Manufacturing Buyer: Roy L. Pickering, Jr.
Printer/Binder: LSC Communications
Cover Printer: LSC Communications

Acknowledgments of third-party content appear on page 161, which constitute an extension of this copyright page.

7 2019

Library of Congress Cataloging-in-Publication Data
Names: Quick, Teri, author. | Zimmer, Melissa, author. | Hocevar, Diane, author.
Title: Making reading relevant : the art of connecting / Teri Quick, Melissa Zimmer, Diane Hocevar.
Description: Fourth edition. | Boston : Pearson, 2018. | Includes bibliographical references and index.
Identifiers: LCCN 2016055295 | ISBN 9780134179216 (pbk.) | ISBN 0134179218 (pbk.) | ISBN 9780134187686 (annotated instructor edition) | ISBN 0134187687 (annotated instructor edition)
Subjects: LCSH: Reading (Higher education)
Classification: LCC LB2395.3 .Q53 2018 | DDC 418/.40711—dc23 LC record available at https://lccn.loc.gov/2016055295

Student Edition
ISBN 10:   0-13-4-17921-8
ISBN 13: 978-0-13-4-17921-6

Annotated Instructor's Edition
ISBN 10:   0-13-4-18768-7
ISBN 13: 978-0-13-4-18768-6

www.pearsonhighered.com

Contents

Preface

Sometimes less is more. In this age of information overload, it seems imperative that students learn to become better, more efficient readers—and not by reading volumes on *how* to read, but by exposure to essential reading strategies with a major focus on application practice. This practice can be done using "real-life" materials (primary reading sources, such as textbooks, newspapers, and magazines) and/or by using a computer-based program. This text addresses all reading topics necessary for success in college reading, as well as those assessed on state-wide reading tests (including Texas and Florida). It's intended for use in any college reading course, from college prep to higher level, within a variety of contexts, which are as follows:

- Reading courses that incorporate primary reading sources, such as newspapers, news magazines, novels, textbooks, and the Internet. Essential reading strategies are presented, but the choice of practice materials should be consistent with the reading level of the course.
- Reading courses that will use this as a stand-alone text.
- Reading courses "paired" or "linked" with a content-area course. Students would use the content course textbook as their primary reading source, and would be truly *"making reading relevant."*
- Paired reading and writing courses or a combination reading/ writing developmental class. When reading is paired with a writing course, this text helps students see the strong connections between reading and writing. It includes a thorough chapter about patterns of organization strategies, which coincides well with most developmental writing courses. The text offers extended writing practice in the Learning Activities sections of the Instructor's Manual, in addition to the "Writing Like a Reader" feature in every chapter.
- Online reading modules or courses. Due to the increasing demand for online courses, the text lessons and Learning Activities (included in the Instructor's Manual) are structured to be easily adapted for the development of online reading modules.
- Reading courses on a quarter system because of the brevity of the text.
- Reading courses on a semester system that focus on the application of strategies using primary reading sources.

FEATURES NEW TO THE FOURTH EDITION

- More academic-oriented examples and readings were added throughout the text.
- Updated vocabulary resources were added to Chapter 1, "Vocabulary Strategies," to incorporate the use of personal electronic devices.
- Chapter 3, "Textbook Strategies," was expanded to include illustrations for Cornell note-taking and textbook annotating.
- Chapter 4, "Critical Reading Strategies," was slightly condensed for clarity, and updated with more current excerpts.
- A short section on idioms was added near the end of Chapter 5, "Figurative Language Strategies," and simpler examples and practices were added to the section on personification.
- In Chapter 6, "Patterns of Organization Strategies," new academic readings were added to provide pattern awareness, understanding, and practice across the content areas. This chapter is designed to help link a reading course as a co-requisite or paired course to any other college-level or developmental-level writing course.
- In Chapter 7, "Visual Literacy Strategies," academic readings were added to provide relevant examples and practice. The KWL Chart was added as an additional visual literacy chart. This powerful reading tool is appropriate for reading at any level.
- Chapter 8, "Information Literacy Strategies," was updated to align with current terms and methods of accessing and evaluating information obtained via the Internet.

ADDITIONAL FEATURES

The text and Instructor's Manual are structured to help students and instructors work through the lessons *quickly* and meaningfully.

Each chapter includes the following:

- Stated Learning Objectives followed by a readiness quiz. The readiness quiz isn't meant to be a true pretest; its purpose is to help gauge the prior knowledge of the students and to serve as a bridge to the chapter.
- Learning strategies with featured *QUICK* Tips to highlight some of the more important strategies
- Practices using a variety of concise real-life content within the text
- Writing Like a Reader feature
- Check Your Learning feature

- Suggested learning activities called "*Quick* Connections" at the end of each chapter

In addition, *Making Reading Relevant*, 4/e, is strongly supported by the following supplements:

Annotated Instructor's Edition (ISBN 0134187687). Includes solutions to the exercises in the student edition and links to helpful resources in the Instructor's Manual.

Instructor's Manual (ISBN 0134187679). Features ideas for teaching the text strategies, extended practice activities, chapter check-up quizzes, Latin and Greek quizzes, and much more. Available for download from the Instructor Resource Center.

Mytest (ISBN 0134187660). Pearson MyTest is a powerful assessment generation program that helps instructors easily create and print quizzes, study guides, and exams. Select questions from the test bank to accompany Making Reading Relevant, 4/e, or from other developmental reading test banks; supplement them with your own questions. Save the finished test as a Word document or PDF, or export it to WebCT or Blackboard. Available at www.pearsonmytest.com.

Answer Key (ISBN 0134187857). Contains the solutions to the exercises in the student edition of the text. Available for download from the Instructor Resource Center.

This text is designed to be consumable. For maximum benefit, students need to actively respond to the passages and practices in the book by reading, writing, annotating, and highlighting as needed. Most reading texts currently available are much longer, more expensive, and require a greater commitment of students' time. We believe that reading courses that stress the use of primary sources for application practice are more effective than courses that have prechosen, often outdated reading selections for application practice.

This text can easily be read outside of class in preparation for classroom practice. The brevity of the text may encourage more (not less) outside reading by today's students, who are often reluctant to read extensively and/or whose busy lives limit time available for homework assignments. When introduced to new concepts, students benefit from instruction that connects the learning to the place(s) in their environments (work, school, home) where they can use it. Real-life materials might include chapters from content area textbooks, current event and editorial resources (such as magazines and newspapers), novels, college catalogs, recipes, written directions, websites, and computer practice. Current brain research indicates that "students are natural learners, are energized by learning, and apparently, love to learn when they can start learning something new from where they are, using what they already know, and can do their own exploring, thinking, and discovering" (Smilkstein, 2003). This research supports the use of active learning using real-life materials to foster authentic and lasting learning.

For several years, we searched for a simple, concise text to use in our reading classes. We didn't find a brief text that addressed all of the topics we wanted to include. Neither did we find anything that stressed the application of reading strategies using primary reading sources and proven computer practice sites as the basis of the content. This text was written to fill those needs.

TO THE STUDENT

How important is reading to you?

As a student, reading serves as a major tool for learning. You probably have discovered that *how well* you read can and will determine the degree of success you achieve in your classes. Whether you're taking courses in business management, nursing, welding, or any other subject area, you'll be required to read for information, to follow directions, to understand what you read, and to think critically.

Whatever your current reading level, you're taking a positive first step in reaching your academic and career goals by taking a reading course. Actually, reading is much more complex than many students realize. Effective reading requires various levels of thinking. While it's necessary to determine what a passage *says,* it's also crucial to interpret what it *means.* Simply recalling facts differs from making inferences. However, both processes benefit from guided practice. Basic reading strategies cover what is obvious and clear in a passage. More challenging reading strategies cover those parts of a passage that require deeper reflection. In the college reading classroom, the instructor may verbally model both the literal and interpretive processes involved in reading a selection. Students should observe this verbalization and then actively participate in the learning process by sharing and discussing their own "reading thinking."

Making Reading Relevant: The Art of Connecting, 4/e, will introduce you to a comprehensive set of reading strategies. You can use these strategies as tools for learning in your college courses and for managing reading tasks you'll meet on the job and in daily living. The text was designed to minimize the number of practice passages so that you can apply the text strategies to real-life reading materials that are interesting and relevant. Good reading is an art, much like playing baseball or playing the piano. A teacher can show you how to hold the bat or how to put your fingers on the keys, but in order for you to hit home runs or become a concert pianist you need to practice. Our hope is that you'll read this text, complete the practices, apply the strategies to real-life materials, and go on to become a highly successful student!

Teri Quick
Melissa Zimmer
Diane Hocevar

Acknowledgments

Making Reading Relevant, 4/e, is dedicated to all of our family and friends who offered encouragement and support.

> ***From Teri, special appreciation goes to:*** The late Tom Markin, my dad, for his lifelong teaching and belief in me.

> ***From Melissa, special appreciation goes to:*** Scott Zimmer, my husband, a true partner. Kaleb and Chloe, my children, who make my world go round. Janet Riordan, my late mother, whose love for reading forged my path. Jennifer Rumer, my sister, whose belief in me sustains me. Jeremiah Riordan, my dad, who saved our lives.

> ***From Diane, special appreciation goes to:*** Bob Mancuso, my late uncle, who encouraged me to become a teacher. The late Joseph (Chic) and Josephine Mancuso, my parents, who taught me so much about life.

Thanks also to the following people for their roles in making the book happen: Nancy Blaine, our editor, for her guidance and support; Amanda Dykstra, our assistant editor, who's amazing and has helped us tremendously; Laura Mann for encouraging us to write the book; and Craig Campanella, our past editor, for his patience and wisdom.

And also thanks to the following reviewers: AnaLaura Gonzalez, Laredo Community College; Agnes Kubrak, Henry Ford Community College; Denise Clay, Fullerton College.

Teri Quick
Melissa Zimmer
Diane Hocevar

One

Vocabulary Strategies

Chapter Preview

Vocabulary Strategies Overview

A. Context Clues
   1. Definition
   2. Example
   3. Contrast
   4. Inference
B. Word Analysis
   1. Root Words, Prefixes, and Suffixes
   2. Latin and Greek
C. Denotation and Connotation

LEARNING OBJECTIVES (LOs)

Upon completion of this chapter, you will be able to:

■ LO1—Define an unknown word by using context clues

■ LO2—Define an unknown word by using word analysis strategies

■ LO3—Use denotation and connotation to determine the author's meaning of a word

A good vocabulary . . .
        always speaks well for you.

Readiness Quiz

Section 1: Match the underlined word on the left to the best definition on the right.

1. _____	Because _hyperactive_ children often become distracted, teachers should provide a calm environment.	**A.** rule by royalty
2. _____	He is _resilient_, not a weak person.	**B.** loud
3. _____	That man drives me crazy; he is so _vociferous_! I wish he would be quiet.	**C.** overactive
4. _____	Queen Elizabeth is the head of England's _monarchy_.	**D.** opposed
5. _____	Instead of supporting me, he is _averse_ to my position.	**E.** able to recover strength

Section 2: Mark each statement below **T** for true or **F** for false.

6. _____ I know how to sound out a word.

7. _____ I know what the Latin root **aqu** means.

8. _____ The connotation of a word is its dictionary definition.

9. _____ The suffix comes at the beginning of a word.

10. _____ Word analysis involves looking at word parts.

VOCABULARY STRATEGIES OVERVIEW

Improving your vocabulary is important to your success in college, as well as to your success in life. In college, you need a well-developed vocabulary in order to comprehend and learn information presented in your textbooks and to write papers that will earn high grades. In life, you need a good working vocabulary that allows you to succeed in your career and communicate well with others. Vocabulary is associated with educational level and intelligence. Most educated, intelligent people have broad vocabularies, and, like it or not, we are often evaluated by our ability to communicate effectively through the use of the oral and written word.

There are two common strategies for finding the meaning of unfamiliar words: context clues and word analysis. This chapter will describe both. A reader can determine the meanings of many words without having to stop to look them up in a dictionary. The use of context clues and word analysis improves reading comprehension and enhances retention of new words because we tend to remember words we figure out for ourselves.

This chapter will also explain the difference between a word's denotative and connotative meanings. It's important to understand how an author uses words to suggest certain meanings or to evoke emotion in the reader. Understanding denotation and connotation will enable you to notice a writer's word choices and more effectively discern what they are meant to convey. Learning and using the strategies in this chapter will get you well on your way to becoming a more capable reader and communicator!

A. Context Clues

Context clues are the words and sentences around a word that can give clues to its meaning. Writers sometimes knowingly use words that may be unfamiliar to their readers. Therefore, they may use other clarifying words or phrases to help with the understanding of new words. These words or phrases are called **context clues**. If readers are aware that such clues often exist in words or sentences surrounding the unknown words, they can save time and improve comprehension. Context clues enable the reader to make valid guesses about the meanings of many unfamiliar words.

Review the chart below for an explanation and example of each of the four main types of context clues.

Now practice using the four clues.

Clue	Explanation	Example
Definition or Synonym	A definition or synonym (i.e., word that means the same) is in the sentence with the word	**Hypochondria is** abnormal anxiety about one's health.
Example	Examples or illustrations that clarify the word's meaning	He has many **idiosyncrasies, such as** the inability to cross a bridge, holding his feet up across a railroad track, and not letting his food touch on his plate.
Contrast or Antonym	The word's antonym, or opposite, appears in the sentence	The bride was **elated** on her wedding day; however, her parents were very heavy-hearted.

(cont.)

Clue	Explanation	Example
Inference or General Sense	You must apply your background knowledge to the information the context offers	The classroom was **commodious** enough to hold 30 desks, 30 computer stations, an entire technology center for the instructor, and several large bookcases.

1. DEFINITION/SYNONYM   Sometimes the context in which an unfamiliar word appears contains a definition in the form of a synonym or a longer explanation. A reader needs to look for a stated definition or synonym in the sentence containing an unfamiliar word.

USING THE CLUE

Read the sentence and circle the definition of the bold-printed word.

1. A **stamen** is the pollen-producing male organ of a flower.
2. Mary **commiserated**, or sympathized, with a friend who had lost her job.
3. To **harass** someone means to continuously annoy him.
4. Those born in the United States have **suffrage** (the right to vote).
5. The study of how people think and learn, **cognition**, is a field that attracts many psychologists.

Look for the following to help locate a definition in the sentence containing an unfamiliar word:

Clues	"refers to," "is defined as," "means," or "is"
Words in italics	Partitions are *dividers* for rooms.
Words set off by parentheses, dashes, or commas	I have a disorder, vertigo, that leaves me feeling dizzy and confused.
Synonyms	My new neighbor is a sot, or drunkard.

QUICK TIP

Commas, parentheses, and dashes often set off a word from its definition.

2. EXAMPLE Writers often use examples to clarify the meaning of unfamiliar words and terms. Examples are vivid illustrations or explanations that define, either by creating familiar images in your mind or by recalling familiar objects, ideas, or situations.

USING THE CLUE

Read the sentence and answer the questions.

1. To get along with your partner, do your share of **chores**, for example, sweeping, dusting, cleaning the bathroom, doing laundry, and putting the dishes in the dishwasher.

   What are the chores? _____

   _____

   What words let you know "here comes the list"? _____

2. Coughing, runny nose, scratchy eyes, red splotches on your skin, and sneezing illustrate a few **ailments** that are usually associated with allergies.

   What are the ailments? _____

   _____

   Ailments must be _____

3. Jim is a **malcontent** because he has such a negative attitude and finds fault with everything.

   What two things do a malcontent do? _____

   _____

4. I would not mind being locked up with a **docile** animal (cat, goldfish), but I would mind a **predatory** (lion, tiger) one!

   What are two examples of docile animals? _____

   Docile must mean _____

5. The museum owner was trying to **authenticate** the portrait from the 1800s and the vase from King Henry's collection.

   What two things were the owner trying to authenticate? _____

   _____

   Authenticate must mean _____

   _____

Example clue words	for example, such as, consists of

3. CONTRAST/ANTONYM Sometimes the context in which an unfamiliar word or term appears contains an antonym, or opposite word, that helps define the word. Look for words like *but*, *on the other hand*, or *however* to signal an opposite word from which you can gain meaning for the unfamiliar word.

USING THE CLUE

Read the sentences and define the words.

1. The climate in the Midwest is never **static**; on the contrary, it changes daily.

    Define static _____

2. In Darwin's day, his theory of evolution was **iconoclastic**, but today many people think it is a reasonable theory.

    Define iconoclastic _____

3. Although he was gone an **eon**, when she saw him, it seemed like only yesterday they had parted.

    Define eon _____

4. Everyone was pleased to discover that the bus driver was **circumspect**, unlike his brother the taxi driver, whose driver's license had been revoked for recklessness.

    Define circumspect _____

5. My teacher has been called **altruistic** because he gave up his professional baseball career to serve as a teacher in a village in Africa. On the other hand, he has been called **egocentric** because he constantly boasts about what he does for others.

    Define altruistic _____

    Define egocentric _____

Contrast clue words	however, on the other hand, in contrast, but, yet, unlike, different

4. INFERENCE/GENERAL SENSE An inference is an informed guess based upon what you already know and the information available. Sometimes you have to make a guess about a word based upon prior knowledge combined with the information given.

USING THE CLUE

Read the sentence and answer the questions.

1. The maniac concocted a **diabolical** plan to end the world.

    Define diabolical _____

2. The elementary teacher's **buoyant** manner made the children feel welcome and at ease on the first day of school.

   Define buoyant _____

3. The **deft** hands of the artist created a beautiful portrait of the queen.

   Define deft _____

4. It was an **enigmatic** situation, and, as the detective, I had to work overtime to put the facts together.

   Define enigmatic _____

5. Living alone for years, the man developed strange and **eccentric** habits.

   Define eccentric _____

QUICK TIP

Read the words and/or sentences around an unfamiliar word to find clues that help you connect meaning to the word.

QUICK TIP

Look for signal words like "for example" (to illustrate), "however" (to contrast), "means" (to define), and "therefore" (to infer).

USING THE CLUES IN PARAGRAPHS

Use context clues to determine the meaning of each underlined word in the following paragraphs.

Advertising for tobacco products is the most <u>pervasive</u> evidence of company efforts to keep their products in the public eye. Full-page ads in magazines and on billboards portray young, healthy, successful, physically fit people enjoying tobacco products in a variety of circumstances ranging from <u>opulent</u> restaurants and apartments to rafting, boating, and wind surfing.

_____   1. pervasive

      a. pertinent   b. common   c. perfected

_____   2. opulent

    a. bizarre   b. cheap   c. expensive

In today's society, all people have the freedom to explore and develop their potential. We each carry with us responsibility to pursue emotional well-being. During our lifetime we each will be faced with choices to grow or choices to <u>stagnate</u>. Our emotional growth depends upon our ability to take active roles in its development.

_____   3. stagnate

    a. commence   b. stand still   c. endure

Addictions <u>evolve</u> gradually, often from very <u>innocuous</u> beginnings. A person who feels unhappy, overwhelmed, threatened, or bored finds an object or behavior that produces a state of being the person desires, or that <u>suppresses</u> what the person wants to forget. <u>Moderate</u> use of these behaviors, for example, having an occasional drink or partying with friends, does not <u>constitute</u> an addiction. Some people, however, reach a point where they can experience security or pleasure only when they are involved with this object or behavior. Withdrawal of the object produces anxiety and despair. At this point, when the person has lost control and cannot function without the object, he or she is considered addicted.

_____   4. evolve

    a. develop   b. shrink   c. evade

_____   5. innocuous

    a. carefully planned   b. harmless   c. mysterious

_____   6. suppresses

    a. contradicts   b. subdues   c. combines

_____   7. moderate

    a. reasonable   b. secluded   c. numerous

_____   8. constitute

    a. contain   b. abolish   c. establish

Key: 1. B, 2. C, 3. B, 4. A, 5. B, 6. B, 7. A, 8. C

How did you do? Were you able to figure out the meaning of the words by using context clues? Being aware of, and looking for, context clues to word meaning is the first step in building a better vocabulary. The second step, word analysis, will be explained next.

B. Word Analysis

Word analysis involves breaking a word into parts to find meaning. When a reader comes across an unfamiliar word, there are several options available: skip the word, stop and look it up in a dictionary, reread the paragraph containing the word and use context clues to try to figure it out, or use word analysis to try to find its meaning. You've just learned how to use context clues, and when you combine those strategies with word analysis, you're well on your way to more effective vocabulary building.

What does "use word analysis" mean? Word analysis is done using two processes in combination. The first one, breaking the word into syllables and looking for familiar prefixes, root words, and suffixes, may already be a familiar step. The other part of the process, looking for Latin and Greek word parts, may be less familiar. If so, this section will explain how to learn and use common Latin and Greek roots to help analyze and bring meaning to unknown words. The two processes, syllabication and looking for Latin and Greek word parts, can be done at the same time to quickly find meaning for an unfamiliar word.

Consider, for example, the word **immovable**. If you don't know this word, you can start by dividing the prefix, root word, and suffix. Thus you would have the prefix **im**, the root **mov**, and the suffix **able**. Think about what each part means. **Im** is a common prefix meaning "not." The root word **mov** is a Latin root meaning "move." The suffix **able** means exactly what it looks like—able to do whatever comes before it. Put the three meanings together and you have *not move able*—or not able to be moved—which is what immovable means.

Many words don't have a prefix, root, and suffix, and many don't contain a Latin or Greek part. Even so, any word can be broken into syllables, which makes it easier to see if there are prefixes or suffixes, or a Latin or Greek part. If there aren't, dividing words into syllables may help with pronunciation. Since our listening vocabulary is much greater than our reading vocabulary, we recognize many more words by sound than by sight. Thus, if readers can pronounce and hear a word, there's a good chance they will recognize the word and know its meaning.

Using context clues in combination with word analysis strategies enables the reader to quickly determine meaning for many words that are unfamiliar when first encountered. Being able to find meaning for unknown words is a great way to increase vocabulary, which in turn increases comprehension.

QUICK TIP

If you don't remember the long and short vowel sounds, ask your instructor to review them. Many college students have forgotten long and short vowel sounds, but you need to know them to be able to pronounce words.

1. ROOT WORDS, PREFIXES, SUFFIXES Once you've divided a word, look at the first and last parts to see if they include a common prefix and/or suffix. Prefixes come at the beginnings of words and change or modify the meaning. Suffixes do the same thing, but they're added at the ends of words. Prefixes generally have more meaning than suffixes. Many suffixes are used to change the tense (*ed* or *ing*), or to show the state or condition of the root word (*ar*, *al*). Other suffixes do carry meaning, such as *able/ible* (able to), or *ful* (full of).

Some of the most common prefixes mean *not*, or the opposite of what the word means without the prefix. You may recognize the ones in the list below:

un	unhappy
in	inadequate
il	illegal
im	immeasurable
ir	irrational
a	asexual

Train yourself to immediately recognize these prefixes and know that they mean *not*, or the opposite of what the word would be without the prefix. Other common prefixes you should immediately register meaning for are *re*—again, *pre*—before, *co* or *con*—together, and number prefixes such as *uni*—one, *bi*—two, and *tri*—three. Studying common Latin and Greek word parts will teach you the meaning of many more prefixes.

The core of a word is the part we call the root. This is the part that has the main meaning. Because many words are made by adding prefixes and suffixes, the root of the word is often in the middle. Most long words are just a root word with several prefixes and suffixes added. That's why breaking words apart can often show you quickly what they mean if you know the meanings of the separate parts. For example, a word like *irreplaceable* may look long and unfamiliar to you. But if you break it into syllables, starting by dividing off the prefixes and suffixes, you end up with this: ir-re-place-able. Look at each of those parts and substitute the meaning for the prefixes, root and suffix, and you see this: not-again-place-able. This is what the word means: not able to place again, or not able to be replaced. Many longer words are just a string of prefixes and suffixes, so separate those from the root word, and you'll see that long words can be easy to pronounce.

As previously mentioned, suffixes come at the end of words, and they also change, or modify, meaning. Suffixes often change the part of speech of the word as well. For example, *dirt* is a noun, but when the suffix *y* is added, *dirt* becomes *dirty*, which is an adjective. Below is a chart of common suffixes that readers need to know in order to use word analysis to help determine the meaning of unknown words.

Noun Suffixes

Suffix	Meaning	Example
-al	act or process of	refusal, removal, approval
-acy, -ance, -ence	state or quality of	privacy, maintenance, eminence
-er, -or, -ist	one who	trainer, protector, chemist
-ism	doctrine, belief	communism, socialism, materialism
-ity, -ty	quality of	simplicity, duplicity, elasticity
-ment	condition of	contentment, resentment, improvement
-ness, -sion, -tion, -dom	state of being	heaviness, concession, transition, freedom

Verb Suffixes

-ate, -en	become	authenticate, enlighten, duplicate
-ify, -fy, -ize, -ise	make or become	solidify, terrify, civilize, expertise

Adjective Suffixes

-able, -ible	capable of being	presentable, certifiable, edible
-ful	full of	meaningful, playful, resentful
-ic, -ical, -al	pertaining to	authentic, mythical, musical
-ious, -ous, -y	characterized by	nutritious, portentous, messy
-ish, -ive	having the quality of	fiendish, brownish, creative
-less	without	endless, fearless, shameless

> # QUICK TIP
>
> Most long words are made up of a root word with added prefixes and suffixes—take words apart to make them easy to define.

Of course, since the root of a word is the basic part with the most meaning, you have to know what the root means to get meaning for an entire word. Some words, called **compound words**, may contain two roots, or two words put together, such as doghouse. Knowing the meaning of the root or roots is where Latin and Greek come into the process of word analysis.

2. LATIN AND GREEK   Because of the far-reaching influences of the ancient Roman and Greek societies, over half of the English language is based on Latin and/or Greek word parts. Learning some of the most common Latin and Greek parts is a fast way to build a better vocabulary. Once you know the meaning of the parts, you will start recognizing them in unfamiliar words, and you will be able to use your knowledge of the word parts along with the context to figure out meanings of unknown words. The Latin and Greek word parts must be memorized (stored in your long-term memory) in order for them to permanently help you with your vocabulary.

> # QUICK TIP
>
> Flash cards are a great way to memorize the word parts and their meanings. Remember to draw pictures on them!

Following are five lists of the most common and widely used Latin and Greek prefixes and root words. There are 20 prefixes or roots in each list. Think of these lists as your Top 100 vocabulary builders. The prefixes and roots need to be memorized and placed in your long-term memory in order for them to be of benefit to you. We suggest learning 20 words a week for five weeks, reviewing all words weekly as they're learned, and taking a final test over all 100 parts. This process will ensure that you'll remember the meanings when you encounter the roots or prefixes in words. Knowledge of these Latin and Greek parts will make a significant improvement in your vocabulary.

Latin and Greek Prefixes

Word Part	Meaning	Examples	
1. anti	against	antiaircraft	antiabortion
2. co, com, con	together	coworkers	conjoined
3. contra, counter	against	contradict	counterclockwise
4. ex	out	exit	extract
5. hyper	excessive	hyperactive	hyperventilate
6. hypo	under, less	hypodermic	hypothyroid
7. inter	between	interrupt	interstate
8. intro, intra	within	introspective	intramural
9. mis	wrong	misspell	mislead
10. multi	many	multiplication	multilingual
11. peri	around	perimeter	periscope
12. post	after	posttest	postoperative
13. pre	before	prenatal	pretest
14. re	again	redecorate	retake
15. retro	back	retro fashions	retrorockets
16. sub	under	subway	submarine
17. super	above	superintendent	superman
18. syn, sym	together	symphony	synchronize
19. tele	far	television	telescope
20. trans	across	transcontinental	transportation

Latin and Greek Number and Negative Prefixes

Word Part	Meaning	Examples	
1. uni	one	uniform	unisex
2. mono	one	monopoly	monolog
3. bi	two	bisexual	bicycle
4. tri	three	tripod	tricycle
5. quadr	four	quadruplets	quadrangle
6. quint	five	quintet	quintuplets
7. penta	five	pentagon	pentameter
8. hex	six	hexagon	hexagram
9. oct	eight	octopus	octagon
10. dec	ten	decade	decimal
11. cent	hundred	century	centipede
12. kilo	thousand	kilometer	kilogram
13. semi	half	semiconscious	semester
14. un	not	unhappy	unconscious
15. in	not	incapable	incomplete
16. im	not	impossible	immovable
17. il	not	illegal	illiterate
18. ir	not	irregular	irrational
19. a	not	asexual	atypical
20. dis	not	discontent	disable

Latin and Greek Roots

Word Part	Meaning	Examples	
1. am, amat	love	amative	amorous
2. ann, enn	year	annual	anniversary
3. aqu	water	aquarium	aquaplane
4. astr	star	astronomy	astrology
5. aud, audit	hear	auditory	audition
6. auto	self	automatic	autobiography
7. bibli/o	book	bibliography	Bible
8. bio	life	biology	biography
9. capit	head	capital	decapitate
10. chron	time	chronological	chronic
11. cred, credit	believe, trust	credibility	credentials
12. cycle	circle, wheel	cycle	bicycle
13. dem	people	democracy	demographics
14. derm	skin	epidermis	dermatologist
15. dict	say	dictate	diction
16. dyn	power	dynamite	dynasty
17. fid	faith	confidence	fidelity
18. frater	brother	fraternity	fraternal
19. gram, graph	write	autograph	telegram
20. greg	flock	congregation	gregarious

Latin and Greek Roots

Word Part	Meaning	Examples	
1. hetero	other	heterosexual	heterogeneous
2. homo	same	homosexual	homonym
3. hydr	water	hydrant	hydroplane
4. loc	place	location	locale
5. log	word, study	biology	apology
6. mal	bad	malnutrition	malpractice
7. man	hand	manual	manicure
8. mater, matr	mother	maternity	maternal
9. metr, meter	measure	thermometer	speedometer
10. mit, miss	send	transmit	missionary
11. mor, mort	death	mortuary	mortality
12. mov, mot, mob	move	motion	mobility
13. pater, patr	father	paternity	patriarch
14. ped	foot	pedestrian	pedicure
15. phil	loving	philosophy	philanthropist
16. phon	sound	phonics	telephone
17. prim	first	primary	primitive
18. psych	mind	psychology	psychiatrist
19. pyr	fire	pyromaniac	pyrotechnics
20. reg	rule	regulations	regulate

Latin and Greek Roots

Word Part	Meaning	Examples	
1. rupt	break	rupture	interrupt
2. scrib, script	write	scripture	inscribe
3. seg, sect	cut	section	bisect
4. sol	alone	solo	solitaire
5. soph	wisdom	sophisticated	sophomore (wise moron)
6. spect	look	spectator	spectacle
7. tard	late	tardy	retarded
8. tempor	time	temporary	tempo
9. the	God	theology	atheist
10. therm	heat	thermometer	thermostat
11. tract	pull	tractor	extract
12. turb	whirl, agitate	disturbance	turbulence
13. urb	city	urban	suburb
14. vac	empty	vacant	vacuum
15. vers, vert	turn	reverse	convert
16. vid, vis	see	vision	video
17. vit, viv	life	vital	vivacious
18. voc, vocat	call	vocal	vocation
19. xeno	stranger	xenophobia	xenobiotic
20. zoo	animal	zoology	zoologist

Once you've memorized the Latin and Greek word parts, you need to be able to apply that knowledge by determining meaning for words containing Latin and Greek parts when you see them in sentences. Let's see how that works. Below are 10 sentences containing a word based on Latin or Greek. Refer to the lists (if needed) and determine the meaning of the words in italics. Then indicate whether each sentence is True (**T**) or False (**F**).

_____   1. *Postoperative* procedures occur before an operation.

_____   2. An *intravenous* needle goes within the vein.

_____   3. A *decade* lasts twenty years.

_____   4. An *illiterate* person is a good reader.

_____   5. Your *audio* system needs a big screen for maximum effect.

_____   6. *Demographics* show statistics about people.

_____   7. A *hydroplane* needs a paved landing strip at least 200 yards long.

_____   8. A *biped* has two feet.

_____   9. An *urbanite* lives in a small town.

_____   10. A *soliloquy* is a speech by one person.

By combining the knowledge of word parts with the context of the sentence, you can see how it's possible to determine meaning. Often you don't need to know the exact meaning of unfamiliar words, but if you get a general meaning, it's enough for comprehension. Let's see how you did. Here are the answers:

1. F, 2. T, 3. F, 4. F, 5. F, 6. T, 7. F, 8. T, 9. F, 10. T

Your instructor may give you more application quizzes that will increase your ability to determine meaning by using context clues, syllabication, and Latin and Greek word parts. In addition to using these strategies, there's another vocabulary concept you should find helpful. It's described next.

C. Denotation and Connotation

There is a difference between how a word is defined in a dictionary— its **denotation**—and what a word may suggest or how it makes the reader feel. The suggested meaning of a word is called the **connotation**, and this meaning is not found in a dictionary. Connotations are learned as we hear words spoken, or as we read how they're used, in context. Connotation may also result from cultural differences, or how words are used in particular cultures.

Due to connotative meanings, many words create a positive or negative reaction in the reader. For example, one dictionary definition of the verb *travel* is "to go from one place to another" (*Webster's New World Dictionary*, 1995). This word and its meaning are neutral in the sentence below, not really evoking a positive or negative response:

He traveled *all summer.*

However, if a writer wanted to create a more positive image, she might say:

He toured *all summer.*

And if she wanted to communicate a more negative image, she could state it this way:

He drifted *all summer.*

It's important for readers to notice a writer's word choices to more fully understand what the writer is trying to convey.

See if you can identify the more positive connotation in each of the following word pairs:

1. smirk   smile
2. aroma   odor
3. lady   female
4. cram   study
5. desire   lust

The more positive words above are *smile, aroma, lady, study*, and *desire*. For more practice on positive and negative words, see Chapter 4, Critical Reading Strategies.

You often hear that the best way to improve your vocabulary is to read, read, read, and this is true! But doing all that reading takes time, and as a college student, your time is limited. The strategies we've included in this chapter are shortcuts that can help you increase your vocabulary quickly. Here are a few other tips to help in your quest for a better vocabulary:

- Use technology!
  - Private computer: When using a private computer, bookmark a dictionary site and have it on your toolbar for quick access. A good one can be found here: www.dictionary.com.
  - Smartphone: Download a free dictionary and thesaurus app. You can find one app with both here: www.dictionary.com/apps
  - Public computer: When using a public computer, use the Google search box. Type your word in the box and press Enter. Google will return the definition as well as a lot more information.

- Electronic readers: Many e-readers, including the Kindle and iPad, have built-in dictionaries that make it as easy as pressing on a word to see the definition.
- 🔊 Click on this symbol to hear the proper pronunciation of the word.
- Use mnemonics (memory tricks) to help memorize word meanings.
- Make flash cards with pictures to help memorize word meanings.
- Keep a vocabulary notebook to record unfamiliar words, meanings, and sentences containing those words.
- Use new words as much as possible. Use it or lose it!

Writing Like a Reader

One of the most important aspects of good writing is word choice. Word choice means exactly that—you **choose** the best words to express your ideas. Think about the reader as you choose each word. Who is the audience for your writing? What is the purpose of your writing—what do you want to convey to the reader? As you increase your vocabulary by becoming a better reader, you will also improve your writing because you will be able to choose words that express exactly what you want to say to the reader. Good writers avoid vague, general language and clichés (overused words and phrases). Good writers have a large vocabulary from which to choose.

Suppose you want to write an essay calling for stronger regulation of offshore oil drilling. Which of the following two paragraphs would be more convincing to the reader?

Oil spills are bad news for birds. The oil harms their feathers so that they freeze to death. Swallowing the oil makes the birds sick.

Oil spills are devastating to coastal birds such as gulls and pelicans. Viscous oil destroys the insulating properties of their feathers, causing hypothermia that can be fatal. The birds inevitably consume some of the oil while grooming, which can lead to ulcers, diarrhea, anemia, and kidney and liver damage.

The second passage helps the reader visualize the harmful effects of oil spills. It makes a much stronger argument because of better word choices. Always keep the reader in mind when choosing words as a writer!

Chapter Summary

Vocabulary Strategies Overview: An educated vocabulary is important to academic, career, and life success. There are several strategies that enable a reader to quickly determine the meaning of unfamiliar words.

Context Clues
- *Definition:* Also called synonym. Look for a definition or synonym that is directly stated in the sentence containing the unknown word.
- *Example:* An example or examples of the word are given; these enable the reader to understand the unknown word.
- *Contrast:* Also called antonym or opposite. There's a word in the sentence that means the opposite of the unknown word. If you know the opposite word, you can figure out the unfamiliar word.
- *Inference:* Also called general sense. Use background knowledge, common sense, and the way the unknown word is used in the sentence to figure out meaning.

Word Analysis
- Knowing how to divide words into parts enables a reader to sound out and pronounce words to gain meaning from what seems to be an unknown word. Dividing a word into parts also shows the reader any prefixes, roots, and suffixes that give meaning.
- *Root words, prefixes, and suffixes:* Over half the English language comes from Latin and Greek. Knowing the meaning of common Latin and Greek word parts is a quick way to expand vocabulary by giving meaning to unknown words containing those parts. Words that have two roots are called compound words.

Denotation And Connotation
- *Denotation:* The dictionary definition of a word.
- *Connotation:* The suggested meaning of a word.

Check Your Learning (Learning Outcomes)

Have you mastered the Learning Objectives (LOs) for Chapter 1? Place a check mark next to each LO that you are able to do.

_____ LO1—Define an unknown word by using context clues

_____ LO2—Define an unknown word by using word analysis strategies

_____ LO3—Use denotation and connotation to determine the author's meaning of a word

Go back and review the sections that cover any LO you didn't check.

Quick Connections—Chapter One

NEWS SOURCE CONNECTION

Choose an article in a newspaper or news magazine to read. As you read, highlight the words you don't know and write each unfamiliar word on a 3 × 5 card.

Using the article context for each word, guess the meaning, and write your guess at the top of the other side of the card. After you finish reading the article, look up the definitions of your words and write the correct meanings under the meanings you guessed. If your guessed meaning is correct, you don't need to write it again; just write "correct" and congratulate yourself for using your context clues well!

TEXTBOOK CONNECTION

Take a textbook from another class and determine where the vocabulary definitions are located. Are they in a glossary? In the margins? At the beginning or end of each chapter? Make a list of each of your textbooks and where in each the vocabulary is located. If there is no vocabulary help, note that you need to keep a dictionary handy while reading that text.

NOVEL CONNECTION

As you survey or preview a course novel, notice unfamiliar words, and make a list of them. Use word analysis (syllabication and pronunciation; Latin and Greek parts) to figure out as many of the meanings as possible. Then look up the meanings in a dictionary, and write the definitions next to the words before you begin reading the novel. You will have created a glossary to go along with your novel!

WEB CONNECTION

Find and bookmark to your personal computer(s) a good dictionary/thesaurus website. Use it often! Two good ones are www.dictionary.com and www.m-w.com.

Two

Basic Comprehension Strategies

Chapter Preview

Comprehension Strategies Overview
A. Identifying Topics
B. Identifying Main Ideas
C. Identifying Details
D. Improving Comprehension

LEARNING OBJECTIVES (LOs)

Upon completion of this chapter, you'll be able to:
- LO1—Identify the topic of a paragraph or reading
- LO2—Identify the main idea of a paragraph or reading
- LO3—Identify the major details in a paragraph or reading
- LO4—Use a checklist to improve comprehension

Comprehension equals understanding . . .
Understanding equals learning.

Readiness Quiz

Choose **T** for true or **F** for false after reading each statement below.

1. _____ Topic and main idea are the same thing.

2. _____ A topic can be stated in a word or two.

3. _____ The main idea tells the point of the entire passage.

4. _____ All of the details are equally important.

5. _____ There may be a main idea for each paragraph as well as for the entire passage.

6. _____ The topic contains supporting details.

7. _____ The main idea may be stated, or you might have to figure it out.

8. _____ I know what the 5 Ws and H are.

9. _____ The topic is longer than the main idea.

10. _____ I know what to do if I'm having trouble comprehending while reading.

COMPREHENSION STRATEGIES OVERVIEW

Comprehension, or understanding, is the ultimate goal of any reader. If a reader doesn't understand what is read, there's no point in reading. Many students say that comprehension is their biggest reading problem. This chapter shows the reader how to break comprehension down into four easy strategies. The first three strategies—being able to identify topics, main ideas, and details—are the key elements of comprehension. This text offers a fourth strategy for improving comprehension—a comprehension strategies chart that shows what a reader can do to remedy specific comprehension problems. Readers who can identify the three key elements of comprehension and who also have a reference chart to address specific comprehension problems should experience excellent comprehension.

A. Identifying Topics

In order to comprehend the meaning of what they are reading, readers must first be able to identify three key elements: the topic, the main idea, and the details. The first of these, **the topic**, is the most basic of the three—the subject of the entire reading. Who or what is the reading about? The topic is very general and can usually be stated in a word or phrase. If a reader is unable to identify the topic, he or she will not be able to comprehend the reading. This lesson focuses on strategies for identifying the topic as the first step to the comprehension of any reading.

Consider the following paragraph:

> The cool-down period is an important part of an exercise workout. The cool-down involves reducing the intensity of exercise to allow the body to recover from the workout. During vigorous exercise such as jogging, a lot of blood is pumped to the legs, and there may not be enough to supply the heart and brain. Failure to cool down properly may result in dizziness, fainting, and in rare instances, a heart attack. By gradually reducing the level of physical activity during a cool-down period, blood flow is directed back to the heart and brain.

What did you just read about? That's the topic of this paragraph. Remember, it's who or what the entire paragraph is about. Did you come up with the topic "cool-down period"? If so, you're right!

QUICK TIP

Force yourself to state what you've read about (the entire reading) in a word or two. This is the topic.

Let's look at another paragraph to see if you can detect an easy way to identify the topic.

> One big difference between high school and college is the amount of studying needed. In high school, most students spend very little time studying outside of class or study hall. But in college, much more studying is required. They say, to be a successful college student, you should plan to spend two hours studying outside of class for every hour you spend in class. Many new college students have a difficult time learning to spend enough time studying.

What is this paragraph about? Did you say "studying"? That's correct, but how did you know? Often the word that expresses the topic will be repeated frequently throughout the paragraph or reading. If you see the same word many times, this is a good clue that the repeated word is the topic.

QUICK TIP

An often-repeated word is a clue to the topic.

Let's see how good you are at identifying topics in paragraphs. Read the following paragraphs and then state the topic on the line below each one. Remember—it should take only a few words to state what the paragraph is all about!

Topic Practice One

1. You may be surprised to learn that the device we call a lie detector does not actually detect lies (Vrij, 2000). What we call a lie detector is really a polygraph (literally, "many writings"), an electronic device that simultaneously senses and makes records of several physiological indices, including blood pressure, heart rate, respiration, and galvanic skin response (GSR)—changes in the skin's ability to conduct electrical current that are associated with levels of perspiration. Computerized scoring systems have been developed for interpreting the results (Olsen et al., 1997).

TOPIC _____

2. School resource officers can benefit law enforcement, school districts, and the community in general. By having the officers in the schools every day, they can open lines of communication between school officials and the law enforcement community. Many times officers and school officials work on the same problems and have to handle the same "bad" kids, but are not able to work closely together for various reasons. The school resource officers help break down these barriers. (Oliver, 2001)

TOPIC _____

3. Whether you are a student, an instructor, a prospective author, or a bookseller, this site is the place to find a host of solutions to today's classroom challenges—ranging from traditional textbooks and supplements to CD-ROMs, companion websites, and extensive distance learning offerings. (Pearson website)

TOPIC _____

4. Few economists doubt that current Bush tax cuts, $290 billion in this year alone, helped stimulate the economy at first. The rebate checks that arrived in the fall of 2001 helped prop up the economy during a dark period, and consumer spending helped the United States make its way to recovery. Now that the economy is improving, the calculus for tax cuts is different. Will cutting taxes further make a meaningful difference to the economy? And even if it does, can we afford to increase the deficit for the sake of tax relief? (Thottam, 2004)

TOPIC _____

Now that you've practiced identifying the topic of a paragraph, do you have any questions about it? If you do, write your questions here to ask your instructor.

_____

Next, let's see if you can identify the topic of a longer passage. Read the following passage and then write the topic on the line at the end.

TOPIC PRACTICE TWO

The more I observe the human condition, the more I'm convinced that boredom is the single biggest factor in the lives of billions of the people who dwell on this little ball of rock and mud. Here in this country boredom and its attendants, depression and unhappiness, are present in what could well be the overwhelming majority of our citizens.

This is again brought home to me when I read of the astronomical salaries we are paying sports figures and media stars. These people can command these salaries because they have the capacity to entertain millions of our citizens who will watch them in person or on TV and in the movies. This audience justifies the players' salaries, which are made possible by payments from promoters and advertisers who use the media to sell tickets and merchandise to the multitudes.

The entertainment industry exists only because it relieves the boredom and brings temporary "happiness" to millions of its customers. This boredom is so deep and so pervasive in our people that they will tolerate even abysmally poor quality entertainment from the producers. Citizens' desires to escape their lives and themselves make them so desperate they will pay large sums of money for even momentary escape from the boredom they endure. (Tom Markin)

TOPIC _____

Remember—identifying the topic is the first step toward understanding, or comprehending, what you're reading. You have to know what you're reading about before you're ready to go on to the second step of comprehension, which is identifying the main idea.

B. Identifying Main Ideas

The term **main idea** has different meanings according to different instructors, and is often confused with the term *topic*. The topic, as you now have learned, is the general subject of the reading. The main idea, on the other hand, is **the point** the reading makes about the topic. The main idea of a passage or reading is the central thought or message. An easy way to understand the difference between main idea and topic is to imagine overhearing a conversation in which you hear your name mentioned often. You know the *topic* of the conversation is you, but you want to know what is being said about you. You probably wouldn't be satisfied until you knew the point they were making about you, or the *main idea*. The same principle applies to reading. The topic is not enough—you also need to know the main idea.

STATED MAIN IDEA   The topic can usually be stated in a word or phrase, while it takes a sentence or a complete thought to state the main idea. Whether you're reading a paragraph or a longer passage, you'll often find one sentence that best summarizes the entire paragraph or passage. This is your main idea statement, which is called a "topic sentence" in a paragraph, or a "thesis statement" if one sentence states the main idea of a longer passage. Since the topic sentence or thesis statement is most often stated toward the beginning of a paragraph or longer reading, look at the first few sentences to see if one seems to be a general statement that makes a point.

QUICK TIP

Topic = General subject (a word or phrase). Example: dogs

Main idea = Point made about the topic. Example: Dogs make good pets.

Topic sentence = Main idea sentence in a paragraph. Example: Dogs are loyal to their owners.

Thesis statement = Main idea sentence in a longer passage. Example: There are several reasons why dogs make good pets.

Reread the paragraph below in which you identified the topic as being "cool-down period." As you read it now, see if you recognize a sentence that states the main idea of the entire paragraph. Remember, this sentence will tell you what point the writer is making about the cool-down period. What does the writer want you to know about the cool-down period once you've finished reading the paragraph?

The cool-down period is an important part of an exercise workout. The cool-down involves reducing the intensity of exercise to allow the body to recover from the workout. During vigorous exercise such as jogging, a lot of blood is pumped to the legs, and there may not be enough to supply the heart and brain. Failure to cool down properly may result in dizziness, fainting, and in rare instances, a heart attack. By gradually reducing the level of physical activity during a cool-down period, blood flow is directed back to the heart and brain.

Did you find the topic sentence, or main idea? It's the first sentence, which tells you that the cool-down period is an important part of a workout. The paragraph then goes on to explain why the cool-down period is important. But what you need to remember is that the cool-down period is important.

Another easy way to locate the main idea is to use the SQ3R (Survey, Question, Read, Recite, Review) textbook-study method, which is discussed in the next chapter. One of the many benefits of using this method is that it often points you to the main idea. When using SQ3R, you form questions from each heading, and often the answer to your question will be the main idea for that section.

Let's say that there was a heading in your textbook above the paragraph you just read that said **Cool-Down Period**. If you were using SQ3R, you'd make a question from that heading. Since most people know what a cool-down period is, the question you might make from that heading would be something like, "What about the cool-down period?" Then the first sentence would tell you what you need to know about the cool-down period—that it's important.

QUICK TIP

The sentence that answers your SQ3R question is often the main idea sentence.

IMPLIED MAIN IDEA   If you can't find a sentence that summarizes the point being made about the topic, the main idea may be only suggested or implied. In that case, **you** need to determine what the main idea is. If there's no stated main idea, determine your own main idea by asking yourself the following three questions:

1. What is the topic?
2. What are the details trying to show?
3. What is the **ONE** point being made about the topic?

The answer to question 3 is the main idea.

Read the following paragraph and see if you can determine the point, or the main idea, that the writer is making.

A news story in Washington, D.C. reports that, of 184 persons convicted of illegal gun possession in a six-month period, only 14
received a jail sentence. Forty-six of the cases involved persons who
had previously been convicted of a felony or illegal possession of a
gun. Although the maximum penalty for such repeaters in the District of Columbia is ten years in prison, half of these were not jailed
at all. A study last year revealed that in New York City, which has
about the most prohibitive gun legislation in the country, only one
of six people convicted of crimes involving weapons went to jail.

(Goldwater, 1975)

Using our three-question method, see if you can answer the following questions:

1. What is the topic of the paragraph? If you determined that it's
   about illegal gun possession, you're right.
2. What are the details trying to show? Did you get the idea that
   people convicted of illegal gun possession aren't punished very
   often? Each of the examples used pointed out the lack of punish-
   ment for those convicted of illegal gun possession.
3. What is the **ONE** point being made about the topic (illegal gun
   possession)? If you concluded that laws against illegal gun possession in the United States aren't being enforced, give yourself an A+!

That's the point, or main idea, that Barry Goldwater was trying
to make. He used examples to give details, but he never stated his
main idea. It was up to you, the reader, to use your skills to determine
the point the writer wanted you to know.

When the main idea is not stated by the writer in a topic sentence, your work as a reader is more difficult; you still need to identify
the main idea in order to comprehend what you're reading. When you
need to figure out the main idea for yourself because the writer has
implied it, rather than directly stated it, remember that it's up to you
to identify the topic, add up the details, and decide what point the
writer is making. In addition to using information stated in the reading, you're also expected to use any background information you
already have about the topic to help determine the main idea. Once
you've done that, if you're reading from material you can write on, it's
a good idea to write the main point in the margin. This will help you
solidify the main idea in your mind, and it will help you when you
review the material at a later date.

If you're not sure you've found the topic sentence, or that you've
made the correct assumption about the main idea, here's an easy way
to check yourself. If most of the details are related to the topic sentence you chose, or if they add up to the main idea you stated in your
own words, then you're probably correct.

QUICK TIP

Most of the sentences in the reading should relate to the main idea. If they don't, you haven't found the correct main idea.

Let's try determining the main idea in paragraphs where there's no topic sentence. Read each of the following paragraphs. Using the details given, plus your background knowledge, determine the main idea for each paragraph and write it on the line below the paragraph. The first paragraph is taken from a dental radiography text, and the second is from a psychology text.

MAIN IDEA PRACTICE ONE

Dental Radiography

The operator should always wear protective eyewear, mask, utility gloves, and a plastic or rubber apron when cleaning the tank or changing the solutions. The tank and its inserts should be scrubbed each time the solutions are changed. A solution made up of 1.5 oz (45 ml) of commercial hydrochloric acid, 1 qt (0.95 L) of cold water, and 3 qt (2.85 L) of warm water is sufficient to remove the deposits that frequently form on the walls of 1 gal (3.8 L) inserts. Commercial solutions for cleaning are available. (Johnson, McNally & Essay, 2003)

MAIN IDEA: _____

Psychology

For nearly a century, researchers have agreed with the proposal that we are sensitive to at least four primary tastes: sweet, sour, bitter, and salty (Henning, 1916; Scott and Plata-Salaman, 1991). Hence it is reasonable to suppose that there are at least four different types (shapes) of receptor sites. The arrangement is like a key fitting into a lock. In this case, the key is the molecule and the lock is the receptor site. Once the sites are occupied, depolarization occurs and information is transmitted through the gustatory nerve to the brain. . . . A number of molecules can occupy a receptor site: The better the fit, the greater the depolarization (McLaughlin & Margolskee, 1994). Keep in mind, however, that the lock-and-key theory is not absolute. Even though a receptor signals a certain taste more than others, it can also contribute to the perception of other tastes (Erickson, DiLorenzo, & Woodbury, 1994).

MAIN IDEA: _____

Whether the main idea is stated in a topic sentence or merely implied, being able to find the main idea in what you read is **crucial** to your comprehension. If you don't know what the writer wants you to know when you're finished reading, you haven't *really* read the material because *reading is comprehension.*

Now that you know how to identify the topic and the main idea, you're two-thirds of the way to good comprehension. Knowing what the reading is about and knowing the main point the author is making are obviously important to comprehension. But you still need more information to comprehend fully, or understand, everything you need to know. The information that gives you complete understanding is contained in the details—the third element key to comprehension.

QUICK TIP

REMEMBER! The main idea for a longer reading might not always be stated in a sentence. If you can't identify a main idea sentence after completing a longer reading, jot down the most important information you remember. Look at your notes for key points. Think about how they are connected. What one idea ties everything together? This is the main idea of the entire reading.

C. Identifying Details

Once a reader has identified the topic and main idea of a reading, the next step to comprehension is to find the details that will fill in and complete your understanding. Most readings have many details; some need to be remembered, others don't.

MAJOR DETAILS   The details that relate directly to the main idea are called major details; these are important and need to be highlighted or recorded in some way. Major details explain, develop, support, and give examples of the main idea. They back up the main idea or offer important new information.

A skilled reader starts to identify the major details by using the 5 W and H questions with the main idea. These questions ask *who, what, when, where, why,* or *how.*

Consider the following paragraph:

Forty percent of children say the American Dream is beyond their reach. A quarter don't feel safe walking alone on the streets of their own neighborhoods. Almost a third of kids under 17 went without health insurance during the last year. Marguerite Sallee, 58, a blond Republican in a power suit, cites these figures to show one thing: America needs to do a better job of caring for its children.

Newsweek magazine, October 3, 2005

To comprehend a paragraph, start by identifying the topic. Here, if you came up with "children" as the topic, you're right. Next, ask yourself what point is being made about the topic, and whether there's a sentence that states it. The last sentence nicely states the writer's main idea. Now you need your major details to complete your comprehension of this paragraph.

Let's try the 5 Ws and H.

Who? <u>Marguerite Sallee.</u>

What? <u>More caring for children.</u>

When? <u>Now (implied).</u>

Where? <u>America.</u>

Why? <u>Examples: American Dream beyond reach, don't feel safe, no health insurance.</u>

How? <u>Not stated in the paragraph, but you would expect the answer in following paragraphs.</u>

With this information, your comprehension of the paragraph should be complete, and you should understand what the writer wants you to know.

QUICK TIP

Start identifying major details by finding the answers to your 5 W and H questions.

After you've identified the most important details by answering your 5 W and H questions, there's another way to find major details if you're reading from a source with headings using SQ3R. Find the answers for your SQ3R questions, which may be different from your 5 W and H questions. The answers to SQ3R questions made from headings may also be major details. The last step is to look for details that directly relate to or support your main idea. If the detail doesn't tie in directly, it's not a major detail.

QUICK TIP

Check a detail against the main idea statement to see if it's a major detail.

MINOR DETAILS   There are other details that could be left out and the main idea would still be clear. These are called minor details. These details explain a major detail. The minor details are used to add interest, but usually don't need to be remembered, and aren't necessary for comprehension.

To illustrate the difference between major and minor details, read the following paragraph and identify topic, main idea, and the major and minor details.

DETAILS PRACTICE ONE

There are a number of ways to get rid of hiccups. The first way, which many people try, is holding their breath and counting to ten. However, most people never make it to ten because the hiccups take over and interrupt the process. Another common method is to try breathing into a paper bag. I had a friend who tried this and it only made his stomach hurt and his hiccups get worse. Finally, there's the method of trying to scare the hiccups away. If you can get someone to sneak up on you and yell, that might make the hiccups stop. Hopefully one of these methods will work for you.

TOPIC: _____

MAIN IDEA: _____

Major Details	**Minor Details**
1. _____	1. _____
2. _____	2. _____
3. _____	3. _____

How did you do? Was it easy for you to see that the paragraph was telling you about three ways to try to get rid of the hiccups? That's what was important. Knowing that most people can't make it to ten when counting, or what happened to the friend, isn't what you need to know or remember from the paragraph. What you need to know to comprehend the paragraph are the major details, or the three ways to get rid of hiccups. Being able to identify the major details that support the main idea is the final piece to the comprehension puzzle.

Now that you've learned the three key strategies for comprehending your reading materials, you should be well on your way to good comprehension! Knowing how to identify the topic, main idea, and major details in your reading material leads to good comprehension. However, there still might be times when you find yourself losing attention and having difficulty understanding what you're reading. The last comprehension strategy addresses what you should do if this occurs.

Writing Like a Reader

Why do you write? You write to share information, thoughts, and ideas with a reader. Think about things you've read that have been difficult to understand—what made it difficult? The most common reason is that the paragraphs were hard to follow. Well-written paragraphs have two aspects that make them easy for the reader to understand: unity and coherence. Unity means that all of the sentences (details) in the paragraph support the topic sentence (main idea). Coherence means that the sentences flow smoothly and logically. The two together create comprehension for the reader. Since comprehension is the end goal for both the reader and the writer, be sure to consider unity and coherence as you write.

To see the difference unity and coherence make, read the following paragraph. Then reread the paragraph in Details Practice One that you just read. Which one is easier to understand? Why?

I had a friend who tried this, but it only made his stomach hurt and his hiccups get worse. If you can get someone to sneak up on you and yell that might make the hiccups stop. Most people never make it to ten because the hiccups take over and interrupt the process. Try breathing into a paper bag. There's the method of trying to scare the hiccups away. Many people try holding their breath and counting to ten. There are a number of ways to get rid of hiccups.

D. Improving Comprehension

The following checklist is a great tool for improving comprehension that goes beyond being able to identify topic, main idea, and major details. Sometimes, you'll find yourself having difficulty comprehending a certain reading and becoming frustrated. That's the time to turn to the Comprehension Strategies checklist. It can help you determine why you're having problems, and how to correct them. To use the checklist, read through the possible problems on the left side. Once you've decided what your problem is, read through the suggestions on the right side and try them until you find a solution that works for you.

Comprehension Strategies

Problems	Strategies
Having difficulty concentrating	1. Take frequent breaks. 2. Read difficult material when your mind is fresh and alert. 3. Use guide questions (see SQ3R section in Chapter 3). 4. Stop and write down distracting thoughts. 5. Move to a quieter place. 6. Stand or walk while reading.
Words are difficult or unfamiliar	1. Use context clues. 2. Analyze word parts—look for Latin or Greek roots that will give meaning for the word. 3. Skim through material before reading. Mark and look up meanings of difficult words. Jot meanings in the margin or on 3 × 5 cards. 4. Use glossary or margin definitions if available.
Sentences are long or confusing	1. Read aloud. 2. Express each sentence in your own words. 3. Look for key words—subject and verb. 4. Break long sentences into shorter sections.
Ideas are hard to understand; complicated	1. Rephrase or explain each in your own words. 2. Make notes. 3. Locate a more basic text or video that explains ideas in simpler form. 4. Study with a classmate, discuss difficult ideas. 5. Search the Internet for simple explanations of the ideas presented in the text.

Ideas are new and unfamiliar; you have little or no knowledge about the topic and the writer assumes you do	1. Make sure you didn't miss or skip introductory information.
	2. Get background information by:
	  a. Referring to an earlier section or chapter in the book
	  b. Referring to an encyclopedia
	  c. Referring to a more basic text
	  d. Referring to the Internet

(cont.)

Problems	Strategies
The material seems disorganized, poorly organized, or there seems to be no organization	1. Read the Table of Contents—it's an outline of the book and each chapter. 2. Pay more attention to headings. 3. Read the summary, if available. 4. Try to discover organization by outlining or drawing a concept map as you read.
You don't know what is important; everything seems important	1. Use surveying or previewing. 2. Ask and answer guide (SQ3R) questions. 3. Locate and underline topic sentences.

Chapter Summary

Topic: General subject of passage; can be stated in a word or phrase.

Main Idea: Point being made about the topic. Stated main idea means that the main idea is directly stated in a sentence. Implied main idea is not directly stated, but is suggested or implied.

Details: Two kinds: major and minor. Major details support the main idea and are important. Minor details are less important and usually don't need to be remembered. Use the 5 Ws and H to find the major details.

Improving Comprehension: Use the Comprehension Strategies chart.

Use the Four Strategies above to Comprehend What You Read.

Check Your Learning (Learning Outcomes)

Have you mastered the Learning Objectives (LOs) for Chapter 2? Place a check mark next to each LO that you're able to do.

_____ LO1—Identify the topic of a paragraph or reading

_____ LO2—Identify the main idea of a paragraph or reading

_____ LO3—Identify the major details in a paragraph or reading

_____ LO4—Use a checklist to improve comprehension

Go back and review the sections that cover any LO you didn't check.

Quick Connections—Chapter Two

NEWS SOURCE CONNECTION

Using a news source (news magazine or newspaper), choose an article to read. Keep in mind that you're looking for the topic, the main idea, and three important details. After reading the article, take three different colored highlighters and highlight the topic in one color, the main idea sentence in another color, and three important details in the third. If the main idea is not stated in a sentence, write your own main idea statement.

TEXTBOOK CONNECTION

Use a textbook from one of your other classes, and if possible, do this activity as you're doing a reading assignment for the other class. Choose a section of the text and write the heading for that section on a sheet of paper. Scan the section for subheadings, and write those below the heading, leaving three lines between each subheading. As you read that section, fill in each of the three lines with an important detail from the section. If you do this for the entire assignment, you'll have a complete set of study notes.

NOVEL CONNECTION

After reading each chapter of a novel, stop to write down the topic of the chapter, the main idea, and at least three major details, or important things that happened. If you're unsure about the topic and/or main idea, write the details first, then see what they all relate to (topic), and what point is being made (main idea).

WEB CONNECTION

Go to a news source website, such as the *Time* magazine site or the *New York Times* newspaper site. Choose an article that looks interesting and skim it to see what it's about. Write down what you *think* the topic and main idea of the article are. Read the article and then review what you initially wrote for the topic and main idea. Decide if your prediction was correct, and if not, rewrite what you now believe to be the topic and main idea. This is a good way to check your comprehension for any article you read.

Three

Textbook Strategies

Chapter Preview

Textbook Strategies Overview

Course information bottom line . . .
The Textbook

LEARNING OBJECTIVES (LOs)

Upon completion of this chapter, you'll be able to:

■ LO1—Identify and use textbook organizational aids

■ LO2—Use three textbook reading methods

■ LO3—Comprehend information found in graphs, charts, and tables

■ LO4—Take notes while reading

■ LO5—Use skimming and scanning

■ LO6—Use a textbook excerpt to practice textbook strategies

Readiness Quiz

Choose **T** for true or **F** for false after reading each statement below.

1. _____ Most textbooks are set up in a similar way.

2. _____ In college, a student needs to read everything thoroughly.

3. _____ I've used highlighting to mark important information in a textbook.

4. _____ The index is the place to find the meaning of words used in a book.

5. _____ I normally read the preface in my textbooks.

6. _____ Skimming and scanning mean about the same thing.

7. _____ A reader who thoroughly reads the material once can remember most of the chapter.

8. _____ I have a method I use when I read textbooks.

9. _____ Scanning is used to get a quick overview of the reading material.

10. _____ When reading from a textbook, a reader should begin on the first page of the chapter and read until the chapter ends without skipping anything.

TEXTBOOK STRATEGIES OVERVIEW

As a college student, it has been estimated that you'll receive approximately 70 percent of the information you need to know from your textbooks. Therefore, it's extremely important that you know how to read your texts, comprehend them, gain the knowledge needed to pass your classes, and ultimately, to be successful in your career.

To achieve your textbook reading goals, there are three simple strategies you can use. The first, identifying and using textbook organizational aids, is simply knowing what the aids are, being aware of them as you start each new textbook, and then using them to assure the most efficient reading of your textbooks. The five textbook aids you'll be learning about in this chapter are the preface, table of contents, glossary, index, and appendix.

The second strategy you'll learn is to use at least one of three methods specifically designed for reading textbooks, which will enable you to get the most out of your book in the least amount of time. By now I'm sure you've discovered that trying to read a textbook the same way you read a novel or a newspaper just doesn't work! Because textbooks are fact dense, and because you're expected to remember much of the material, it takes an entirely different approach to read a textbook. Most readers have never been taught how to read textbooks. This results in a high rate of frustrated students and teachers. In this chapter, you'll learn three methods for reading textbooks that are easy and really work! Because students have different learning styles, we've included three methods: SQ3R (Survey, Question, Read, Recite, Review), 5C (Connect, Cards Vocabulary, Cards Main Points, Classroom, Commit to Memory), and triple highlighting. One of the methods, or a combination of them, will likely work for you.

The third textbook strategy that every college student can benefit from is a combination of two processes: skimming and scanning. You'll learn how to do both, and you'll also learn when to use these time-saving techniques.

Knowing and using the textbook strategies in this chapter can definitely make you a more successful college reader. Take the time to learn and practice these strategies until they become automatic. You'll be amazed at how much easier reading and comprehending your texts will become!

A. Identifying and Using Textbook Organizational Aids

There are five common parts of a textbook (called organizational aids) that can make you a more efficient textbook reader. The five organizational aids in a text that are most useful to the student are the **preface** (also called To the Student), **table of contents**, **glossary**, **index (indexes)**, and appendix **(appendices)**. In addition to knowing these five parts, it's important to check each textbook for other textbook aids such as chapter previews and reviews, chapter objectives, summaries, headings and subheadings, visual and graphic aids, margin information, chapter questions, and vocabulary aids.

QUICK TIP

Always read the preface or To the Student section of your texts to quickly see what aids the author has included that will help you use that text more efficiently.

Your instructor may have you participate in an activity that will allow you to discover for yourself the five parts of a text mentioned above, and how each part can help you use your textbooks more efficiently. If your instructor chooses not to use the following activity with your class, complete it on your own with a text, or several texts, available to you.

QUICK TIP

Start every school term by looking through each of your new textbooks to familiarize yourself with the five textbook organizational aids.

Textbook Organization and Aids

After being divided into groups and assigned one of the five text parts below, work as a group to fill in your section with a description of that part of a textbook. List the kinds of general information that would be found in that part of any textbook, not information specific to the text you're using. Complete your assigned part with your group and then fill in the others as each group presents.

Preface

_____

_____

_____

_____

_____

_____

Table of Contents

_____
_____
_____
_____
_____

Glossary

_____
_____
_____
_____
_____

Index(es)

_____
_____
_____
_____
_____

Appendix (Appendices)

_____
_____
_____
_____
_____
_____

Other Textbook Aids

_____
_____
_____
_____
_____

B. Textbook Reading Methods

Reading a textbook is like playing a football game. You would never be able to win the game if all you did was show up and play. There's much time spent before the game preparing, there's a plan for the actual playing time, and there's follow-up to make sure you learn from that game so you can do better in the next one. In order to "win" at reading textbooks, you need a plan that includes pregame preparation, playing strategies, and postgame follow-up.

We've included three different game strategies, or textbook reading methods. You'll notice that each has a pregame (prereading) step, a playing (reading) plan, and a postgame (review) follow-up. Try each of them and see which one works best for you. You may want to combine parts of all three and come up with your own. What's important is that you have a method that works for YOU. Don't just show up to read and be a loser at the textbook reading game. Get your game plan, use it for every reading assignment, and be a winner at college textbook reading!

Here are brief explanations of the three text strategies. After you've read through them and have a basic understanding of how each one works, your instructor will provide you with several activities so you can try the strategies and determine which one, or which combination of the strategies, works best for you.

1. SQ3R (SURVEY, QUESTION, READ, RECITE, REVIEW)   **SQ3R** has been one of the most popular text-reading strategies since World War II, when it was widely used by soldiers to learn the material in their training manuals. Many studies have been done on the effectiveness of SQ3R, all showing that students comprehend and retain more information when using SQ3R. SQ3R is an excellent textbook reading method for most students because it's easy to use and it works! It works because it makes you *think* about what you're reading. Here's a brief explanation of the five steps in the SQ3R method.

Survey

Purpose: To become familiar with the overall content and organization of the material before you start reading. This enables you to comprehend faster and more thoroughly.

Method: Survey or preview the material by reading and **highlighting** the following:

- Title and subtitle
- Introduction (this can take several forms—chapter overview, chapter preview, chapter highlights, a list of main points in the chapter, or simply a paragraph)

- Headings and subheadings
- Bold or colored print, italics
- Margins
- Boxes
- Graphics (e.g., pictures, charts, graphs, diagrams, tables—and their captions)
- Vocabulary definitions
- Summary—End of chapter, end of sections—any summaries
- Questions—End of the chapter or sections—any questions
- Anything that catches your eye!

Result: A good survey gives you all of the most important information in a chapter and shows you how it's organized. This allows you to start comprehending as soon as you start to read.

QUICK TIP

Surveying, plus reading once, has been proven more effective than reading a selection twice. Don't skip the survey!

Question

Purpose: To give you something to think about before you start to read a section, and to give you something to look for as you read— the answer to your question. If you're looking for an answer, you stay more focused on the meaning of what you're reading.

Method: Make a question from each heading and subheading by using one of the W or H words (who, what, where, when, why, how). Write your W or H word lightly by the key word(s) in the heading. Most often your question will probably be "what is . . . ?" and then the heading. Your question should ask about the aspect of the heading that you're most curious about.

Result: You've created interest and now have a purpose for your reading—to find the answer to your question. Reading with interest and a purpose results in better attention to the content and improved comprehension.

> ## QUICK TIP
>
> Use the 5 Ws and H to form questions from the headings.

Read

Purpose: To gain information and knowledge by finding the answer to your question.

Method: Read through the section under the heading looking for the answer to your question. Read only until you come to a new heading, then stop.

Result: You find the answer to your question, and your mind doesn't wander like it does when you read without a purpose. Also, you should understand and remember what you read because you're paying attention to it.

Recite (Highlight)

Purpose: To get a permanent record of the information you need to remember.

Method: Start by reciting (saying) and then highlighting the answer to the question you made from the heading. Recite and highlight names, dates, definitions, key parts of topic sentences, lists—everything you think might be on a test. After you've highlighted key information, you may also want to write yourself some notes in the margin to clarify certain passages or to remind yourself of things you need to memorize or things you need to ask your instructor. Remember that the key to good highlighting is never to try to highlight as you read material for the first time. Wait until you finish a section, then go back and highlight using the suggestions above.

Result: You now have a permanent record of the information you need to study for the test. From this point on you'll only reread what you've highlighted, so make sure you think your highlighting is accurate and complete. If you aren't able to, or don't want to highlight in the book, use one of the alternative methods of recording such as taking notes, outlining or mapping (Chapter 7), or try the 5C method, which is explained next.

QUICK TIP

Read only from one heading to the next, and then STOP. Go back over what you just read and highlight the answer to your question plus any other important information.

Review

Purpose: To learn the material you need to know.

Method: Reread your highlighting at least three times. The first time to review is as soon as you've completed the reading. Check your highlighting at this time to make sure it's complete and accurate. The second time to reread your highlighting is every week, if possible, but at least once between finishing the assignment and starting to study for the test. The third time is before the test. Start rereading your highlighting several days before the test, and continue until test time. Also, memorize anything that you must have committed to from memory.

Result: You know everything you need to know from the text, and are ready to do well on your test.

QUICK TIP

Reviewing is easy—just reread your highlighting and margin notes! The more often you read over them, the less studying you'll need to do right before a test.

While SQ3R does not require the use of index cards, it may be helpful to students to include cards in the process. The following chart provides that option. Note the asterisks (*) both within the top two boxes of the chart and in the explanations below the chart.

SQ3R with Cards at a Glance

Step 1: Survey*	Go through the chapter: Read title, headings, and subheadings; **look at** and **read** captions for all pictures, charts, and graphs; note anything that stands out such as bolded vocabulary; read chapter overview, summary, and questions at start and/or end of chapter.
Purpose	To connect with prior knowledge, and to get an overview of chapter content and organization.
Result	You get more out of your reading when you do read the chapter, and you retain more of what you read.
Ask Yourself	Do I have a good idea of what this chapter is about and how it's organized?
	Do I have some background knowledge from previous experiences?
Step 2: Question**	Turn the title and each heading into one or more questions using the 5 Ws and H (who, what, why, where, when, and how); write questions above each heading or on a 3 × 5 card.
Purpose	To create interest and read with a purpose; to stay more focused on the content.
Result	You're better able to locate main ideas and major details.
Ask Yourself	Did I turn the title and all headings into appropriate questions?
Step 3: Read	Read from one heading to the next, looking for the answers to your questions.
Purpose	To locate and to begin to learn the chapter content.
Result	You find answers to your questions, stay more focused, and experience better comprehension.
Ask Yourself	Did I notice that reading with a purpose helped me to better understand the reading?

*VOCABULARY CARDS: (Complete this step right *after* the SURVEY step.)

• Identify key words in chapter which are bold-faced and/or listed.
• Make a 3 × 5 (or larger) card for each word; place word on one side of card and the definition on the back side.
• Add any pictures or other personalization (such as colors, shapes, designs) to each card.

**COMPREHENSION CARDS: (Complete this step as you complete the QUESTION step; add your questions by each heading.)

• Identify chapter sections using main headings for the divisions; determine how many sections the chapter includes.
• Write main headings and all subheadings on 3 × 5 (or larger) cards for each section. This will look like an outline of the section. Write on only one side of cards. If more space is needed per section, staple cards together. Each section is one CHUNK of information.

(cont.)

Step 4: Recite/ Highlight	AFTER reading each section, highlight the answers to your questions in the text OR write the answers in the margin of the text or on the same cards you used for the questions.
Purpose	To gain information by finding the answers to your questions.
Result	You have a better understanding and retention of information as well as a record of what you need to know for a test.
Ask Yourself	Did I find and mark or write the answers to the questions I formed in Step 2?
Step 5: Review	Reread your highlighting, notes, or cards as soon as possible, and then periodically and before a test.
Purpose	To move information from short-term to long-term memory, and to effectively prepare for a test without cramming.
Result	You learn the material you identified as important and perform well on the test.
Ask Yourself	Has this method helped me to learn my chapter information and commit it to memory?

2. 5C **5C** was developed to give students a different way to break down and comprehend textbook material. This method uses 3 × 5 note cards, rather than highlighting, to record important information. It is based on the idea that the vocabulary and headings provide most of the key information in a textbook reading. There are times when you can't, or prefer not to, highlight in a book. Having your information on cards also makes studying more convenient because you can carry the cards with you and read over them whenever you have a few minutes of extra time. Hundreds of students have used 5C with a high degree of success.

Connect

Purpose: To connect with the content and organization of the chapter.

Method: Go through the chapter (it takes approximately 10–15 minutes) and **look at** and **read** everything that catches your eye. This will include the title, headings, bold or color print, boxes or items in the margins, captions for all pictures, and charts and graphs. Skim (quickly read for main points) the summary and questions at the end of the chapter.

Result: This step will make it quicker and easier for you to comprehend because you'll get a good idea of what the chapter is about and you can start relating your background knowledge to the chapter content.

Cards Vocabulary

Purpose: Much of the key information in a chapter is contained in the vocabulary words. Use 3 × 5 note cards to identify and define vocabulary words.

Method: Go through the chapter and write each vocabulary word on a separate card and write the definition on the other side. In addition to the definition, writing a sentence containing the word will help you understand and remember the meaning of the word.

Result: You have a set of note cards containing the key vocabulary terms and definitions from the chapter.

Cards Main Points

Purpose: The other source of key information in a chapter is headings. Use 3 × 5 note cards to write questions and answers from the headings. This results in better comprehension and a record of the important information.

Method: Go through the chapter and outline the information on cards using the font size of the headings. The chapter title will be the largest. The next size down will be the main points, the next size down will be the major details, and the next size down will be the minor details. Use colors to separate your outline. When you outline, make sure only one "chunk" of information goes on each card. One chunk would be one main point with its major and minor details. When you come to a new main point, it is time to start another card. If you have a section that takes up two cards, staple those cards together as one "chunk" of information.

Result: You have a set of note cards containing the main points from the chapter.

QUICK TIP

Draw a simple picture on the front (word and question) sides of your cards. The picture should be something that will trigger your memory of the definition or answer to your question. Your mind will remember the picture, and then the answer!

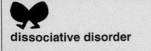

dissociative disorder

characterized by a person having a disruption, split, or breakdown in his or her normal integrated self

Classroom

Purpose: To add information to your cards from your teacher's lecture.

Method: Take your cards with you to class and add important points from your instructor. If there's too much information to fit on your cards, add more cards and staple them to the original cards. Keep all chunks of information about the same main points together.

Result: You now have a complete set of cards that contain the important information from the textbook and from your teacher.

Commit to Memory

Purpose: To learn the information for a test, for future courses, and/or your career.

Method: Carry your cards with you and read through them often. Take them out to review whenever you have a few minutes of time—while waiting, during slow time at work, during TV commercials. Get in the habit of pulling out your cards several times a day!

Result: Frequent reading of the cards and self-testing will commit the information to your long-term memory and is easier and more effective than last-minute cramming.

QUICK TIP

Get in the habit of carrying your cards with you wherever you go and remember to read through them any time you have a few extra minutes. Painless and efficient studying!

5C Method at a Glance: Chapter-Card-Card-Classroom-Commit

Step 1: Chapter	Go through the chapter: **look at** and **read** the captions for all the pictures, charts, and graphs.
Purpose	In order for new information to stick in your brain, you need to access your background knowledge . . . things you already know about a topic.
Ask Yourself	Do I have a good idea of what this chapter is about? Do I have some background knowledge from previous experiences?

(cont.)

Step 2: Cards Vocabulary	On 3 × 5 note cards, create a list of the vocabulary words with their definitions. Add a picture of the DEFINITION to the front of your card for memory and understanding.
Take It a Step Further	Personalize your note cards. Add pictures, shapes, color, and designs. This helps both sides of the brain work together to retrieve information.
Purpose	The main points of your chapter center around the vocabulary. In the next step, you'll see that a lot of the reading has already been done by defining the vocabulary words on your note cards. You'll recognize that the vocabulary words are actually parts of the main points.
Ask Yourself	Do I see how my vocabulary and main points go together in helping make the chapter information clear?
Step 3: Cards Main Points	**Outline your chapter using font size!** The title will be the largest. The next size down will be the main points, the next size down will be the major details, and the next size down will be the minor details. Lots of textbooks use color as a way of distinguishing main points from major and minor details.
Purpose	You aren't expected to remember every written word within your chapter. Matter of fact, you're only expected to remember, or have an idea of, the main points and major details.
Ask Yourself	Did I notice that most of my main points were explained through the vocabulary definitions?
Step 4: Classroom	Bring your cards to class! Take notes on your cards! That is it!! You'll be amazed at how much of your instructor's lecture you'll already know.
Purpose	This keeps points of key information from your text and your teacher together. If you need to create a new card, make sure you staple it to the textbook card so all CHUNKS of information stay together and organized.
Ask Yourself	Do I recognize chapter words in my instructor's lecture?
	As my instructor brings up various topics from the chapter, am I able to locate a note card I created?
Step 5: Commit	Use your cards to study. Your information will be in chunks, therefore making it easier to remember.
Purpose	The brain loves many things, so it's important to remember when actively reading that the brain loves color, repetition, small organized chunks, and design.
Ask Yourself	Has this method helped me to learn my chapter information and commit it to memory?

3. TRIPLE HIGHLIGHTING **Triple highlighting** is a method that has been successfully used in college classes and the military. Air Force trainees using triple highlighting were able to score at least 95 percent on a 100-question, closed-book test. Students in college classes found that the triple-highlighted areas accurately predicted quiz questions. Triple highlighting can be used with SQ3R and 5C if desired, or it can be used by itself. If you like triple highlighting better than the other two methods, be sure you still do some kind of survey, preview, or connection before you start reading. Also review and commit to memory the triple-highlighted areas before a test. Here are the three steps in the triple-highlighting method.

Yellow Highlight

Purpose: To record what you determine to be important information in the chapter.

Method: As you read, use a yellow highlighter to mark what you believe is important information.

Result: You have a record of the information you, the student, have determined to be important.

QUICK TIP

Don't try to highlight as you're reading for the first time. Wait until the end of a section, then go back and highlight the important points. Everything seems important as you're reading—it's easier to see what's important when you have the complete picture.

Blue Highlight

Purpose: To record answers to questions posed by the author at the end of the chapter.

Method: If there are questions at the end of the chapter, find the answer to each question. With a pencil, write the number of the question in the margin next to the answer, then highlight the answer with blue.

Result: You have a record of the information the author has determined to be important.

Pink Highlight

Purpose: To record important points made by your instructor.

Method: Follow along in your text during class lecture and discussion. Notice when your instructor repeats points or writes them on the board. Highlight this information with pink.

Result: You have a record of the information your instructor has determined to be important.

Triple Highlight

Purpose: Shows you which information is most important and most likely to be on your tests.

Method: Reread everything that you've highlighted with all three colors. These areas contain the key information in the reading. The student (you!) thought it was important enough to highlight, the author thought it was important enough to write a question about, and the instructor thought it was important enough to emphasize in class. This means the likelihood of seeing that piece of information again on a test, or in some graded form, is very high.

Result: You have the most important information triple highlighted and ready to study for the test.

QUICK TIP

Research has shown that triple-highlighted information shows up on quizzes and tests a high percentage of the time.

Triple Highlighting at a Glance

Step 1: Survey	Go through the chapter: Read headings; **look at** and **read** the captions for all the pictures, charts, and graphs; read chapter summary and questions.
Purpose	To become familiar with content of the reading.
Result	Shows you the most important points; helps you understand the organization of the chapter; activates your prior knowledge; comprehension begins as soon as you start reading.
Ask Yourself	Did I notice the same ideas repeated in the headings, chapter summary and questions at the end of the chapter? Do I have a good idea of what the chapter is about and how it's organized?

(cont.)

Step 2: Yellow Highlight	Use a yellow (or whatever color you want) highlighter. As you finish each section of the chapter, go back and highlight what YOU think are the most important points.
Purpose	To record what you think is the most important information in the chapter.
Result	You now have a record of what **YOU** think are the main points from the reading.
Ask Yourself	Did I highlight answers to questions I made from the headings? Did I highlight vocabulary words? Did I highlight the 5 Ws? Did I highlight points that I think will be on a test over the reading?
Step 3: Blue Highlight	If your textbook has questions at the end of the chapter, or anywhere in the chapter, scan back over the reading and find the answers to the textbook questions. Highlight the answers in blue (or any color different from your first color). Write the number of the question in the margin in pencil next to the answer you highlighted.
Purpose	To record what the author thinks is important in the chapter.
Result	You now have a record of what **THE AUTHOR** thinks are the main points from the reading.
Ask Yourself	Did I find the answers to all of the chapter questions? Were the answers to the questions already highlighted in my first color? If so, that means you did a good job of choosing important information to highlight in your first color.
Step 4: Pink Highlight	Take your textbook to class with you. When your instructor starts lecturing over the book, use a pink (or any color different from the first two you used) highlighter to highlight information the teacher is talking about or writing on the board.
Purpose	To record what your instructor thinks is important in the chapter.
Result	You now have a record of what **YOUR INSTRUCTOR** thinks are the main points from the reading.
Ask Yourself	Am I highlighting information that is already highlighted in one or two colors? Is my instructor giving new information that's not in the book? If so, you need to be taking notes in addition to highlighting.

(cont.)

Step 5: Triple Highlighting	Reread everything that is triple highlighted as soon as you can after class. Continue to reread the triple-highlighted sections often.
Purpose	You're learning the important information from the chapter. You're also learning what you'll need to know for the test.
Result	You'll earn a good grade on the test. Everything that is triple highlighted is almost guaranteed to show up on the test!
Ask Yourself	Has this method helped me to identify and learn the important information from my reading? Did I make a good grade on the test after using this method? If so, triple highlighting is an effective textbook reading method for you!

Writing Like a Reader

One of the best ways to check and reinforce what you've learned from reading a textbook is to write a summary. You can stop and summarize after every paragraph, every heading, every section, or at the end of the chapter. The ability to write an effective summary is one of the most important writing skills a college student can possess. In a writing course the ability to write an effective summary is important when summarizing information from various sources for a research paper.

A summary has two key features: (1) it is shorter than the original and (2) it repeats the key ideas using different phrases and sentences. A summary must be written using the writer's own words without copying directly from the source. (Copying directly from the source is called plagiarism and is not acceptable. You can learn more about plagiarism in Chapter 8.)

To summarize any type of reading, read a section, then close the text and write the most important information from memory. When you've finished, skim that section again to make sure you didn't leave out any key points. Add anything important that you forgot, and then move on to read the next section. Below is an example summary for the section on Triple Highlighting in this chapter.

Triple highlighting is a textbook reading method that uses three different colors of highlighters. One color highlights what the reader thinks is important. A second color highlights what the teacher says is important, and a third color highlights answers to questions at the end of the chapter. The most highlighted parts of the text are the most important and will probably be on the test.

C. Reading Graphs, Charts, and Tables

Graphs, charts, and tables are pictures of information. You've heard the expression "A picture is worth a thousand words." This is certainly true in reading. The picture provided by a graph, chart, or table can enable readers to see information more quickly than having to read a paragraph or more. Graphs, charts, and tables are often a summary of written text, but sometimes they present additional information. Either way, they are extremely important to the reader, so you need to know how to efficiently read graphs, charts, and tables.

Charts, including graphs, are graphic representations of information. Tables are lists of items. There are common elements involved when reading all three.

1. Read the title.
2. Read the labels.
3. Determine what type of information is being presented.

BAR AND LINE GRAPHS   A bar graph is a visual display used to compare groups of data and to make generalizations about the data.

Example   Given the graph "Enrollment in Introductory Courses at Union University," answer the following questions:

1. Which course has the most students enrolled in it?

2. Order the courses by enrollment from lowest to highest.

3. The enrollment in Econ is approximately how many times larger than the enrollment in Chem?

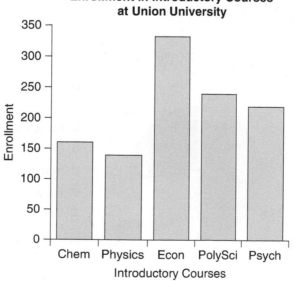

4. Approximately how many students were enrolled in the course with the most students?

5. Approximately how many more students are in Econ than in Physics?

Answers to Example

1. Which course has the most students enrolled in it?

   Answer: Econ

2. Order the courses by enrollment from lowest to highest.

   Answer: Physics, Chem, Psych, Poly Sci, Econ.

3. The enrollment in Econ is approximately how many times larger than the enrollment in Chem?

   Answer: 2 times larger

4. Approximately how many students were enrolled in the course with the most students?

   Answer: approximately 340 students (Econ)

5. Approximately how many more students are there in Econ than in Physics?

   Answer: approximately 200 more students in Econ than in Physics.

CIRCLE GRAPHS   A circle graph is used to show how a whole amount is broken into parts. The whole circle (or pie) graph depicts the entire sample space. The pieces of the pie in the circle graph are called sectors.

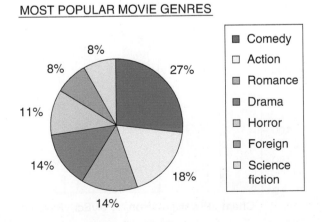

MOST POPULAR MOVIE GENRES

CHARTS   Charts are graphic interpretations of data.

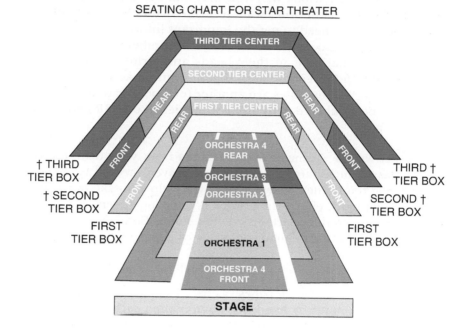

SEATING CHART FOR STAR THEATER

TABLES   Tables are lists of items organized into columns and rows, such as bus or train schedules.

Candy Sold Table

Candy Sold	M	T	W	Th	F	Sa	Su	Total
M&M's	10	9	10	8	12	12	7	68
Snickers	12	11	14	6	13	16	12	84
Mars	15	17	20	14	18	20	15	119
Twix	14	15	18	10	8	18	16	99
Milky Way	13	14	10	8	14	19	9	87
Kit Kat	9	10	12	8	7	12	0	58
Total	73	76	84	54	72	97	59	515

Remember: Reading graphs, charts, and tables is easy:

- Read the TITLE.
- Read the LABELS.
- Determine what type of information is being presented.

D. Taking Notes While Reading

There are several reasons why you may want to take notes while reading. If you can't or don't want to make marks in a textbook or other sources, you need to get the important information recorded on paper. Many students find that they comprehend material better if they summarize it in their heads and write the important points. Written notes can be kept together in a notebook for easy studying later. Written notes are another textbook reading strategy which may be combined with other strategies like SQ3R and triple highlighting.

1. CORNELL NOTES   To make written notes from your textbook or from a classroom lecture, a popular and proven method is Cornell Notes. Using the Cornell Notes method will help you take organized notes without much effort. The Cornell note-taking system divides an 8.5 × 11 page into three sections: (1) Key Points Column (left side of page), (2) Note-Taking Column (right side of page), and (3) Summary (bottom of page).

Here are the steps for using the Cornell Notes method.

1. Set up your note-taking pages:
   - If taking notes by hand, start by dividing each page in your notebook into three parts. Draw a dark horizontal line about five or six lines from the bottom. Use a marker or go over the line several times with your pen so the line is clear and easy to see.
   - Draw a dark vertical line about 2 inches from the left side of the paper from the top to the horizontal line.
   - If taking notes on a laptop computer, you'll find a template online by typing "Cornell Notes template" into a search box.
   - Place the text or course name, date, and topic at the top of each page.
2. Write the notes:
   - The large box to the right is for writing notes.
   - Skip a line between ideas and topics.
   - Don't use complete sentences. Use abbreviations whenever possible. Develop shorthand of your own, such as using "&" for the word *and*.
3. Review and clarify the notes right after reading, or as soon as possible after class:
   - Determine main ideas, key points, dates, and people; then write these in the left column.
4. Write a summary of the notes at the bottom of each page:
   - Use your own words to write a summary of the main ideas in the bottom section.

Psych 101   oo/oo/oo

Theories Abt Love & Loving

John A. Lee	Lee's styles of loving John A. Lee (Canadian, 1973) 4000 statements - 100's of works - fiction, non-fiction
6 styles of love	30 item questionnaire - from responses came up w/ 6 basic styles of loving ① eros ② mania ③ ludus ④ storge ⑤ agape ⑥ pragma
EROS love of beauty total togetherness	① Eros - love of beauty powerful physical attraction love @ first sight - everything together totally into each other
MANIA obsessive low self-esteem	② Mania - obsessive, jealous, possessive, very dependent, need for attention, signs of affection. Associated w/ low self-esteem
LUDUS for fun casual sex no commitment	③ Ludus - carefree, casual - for fun NO COMMITMENT! Not jealous or demanding. Have sex for fun. May have several partners at one time

John A. Lee   6 styles of Love
EROS, MANIA, LUDUS, STORGE, AGAPE, PRAGMA
EROS - beauty, love at 1st sight, togetherness
MANIA - sick, jealous, possessive
LUDUS - no commitment, casual sex

---

5. Study your notes for a test:
   • Reread your notes in the right column.
   • Then, spend most of your time studying the ideas in the left column and the summary at the bottom. These are the important ideas and will probably include most of the information you need to know for a test.

2. ANNOTATION Another way to find and document important information in a textbook is to use annotation. Annotation is simply marking and writing notes directly in a textbook. The purpose of annotation is to be actively involved in your reading. Here are some of the techniques you can use to annotate your text.

- Underline important terms.
- Circle definitions and meanings.
- Write key words and definitions in the margin.
- Signal where important information can be found with key words or symbols in the margin (TQ = test question; * = important; RR = reread, etc.).
- Write short summaries in the margin at the end of major sections.
- Write a question in the margin next to the section where the answer is found.
- Indicate steps in a process by writing numbers next to each step or in the margin.
- Note anything that you don't understand or that you want to ask your instructor.

See the example at the top of the next page for an example of text annotation.

3. HIGHLIGHTING   Highlighting is one of the fastest and most efficient ways to separate important information in a textbook chapter. Of course you can't highlight in a book that doesn't belong to you, but in college an advantage of buying your textbooks is that highlighting is a method you can use if you choose. Highlighting may look easy, and it is if you remember the following points:

a. NEVER highlight as you're reading for the first time. Read through an entire section, or from one heading to the next; then go back and highlight. It will be much easier to determine what to highlight once you have an overview of the information.
b. Here is a list of things to highlight:
    - Answers to your heading questions (if you're using SQ3R)
    - Anything that stood out in your survey or preview
    - Answers to chapter questions (which were read as part of your survey)
    - Topic sentences
    - Main points
    - Names, dates, events
    - Lists (number them too if they aren't already numbered)
    - Anything you think you may be asked on a test
c. Review by reading **just** your highlighting. You don't need to reread everything!

4. "STICKY" NOTES   This note-taking method is an alternative to taking notes directly in a textbook or on notebook paper. As you read assigned textbook material, write key terms and important facts, concepts, or ideas on the "sticky" notes. Then place these notes on appropriate

4 Kinds of love Chapter 3 • Textbook Strategies   **67**

(1) Ludus   **Ludus** is carefree and casual love that is considered "fun and games." Physical appearance is less important to ludic lovers than self-sufficiency and a nondemanding partner. They try to control their feelings and may have several lovers at one time. They are not possessive or jealous, primarily because they don't want lovers to become dependent on them. Ludic lovers have sex for fun, not emotional rapport. In their sexual encounters they are typically self-centered and may be exploitive because they do not want commitment, which they consider "scary."   *no commitment!*

(2) Storge   **Storge** (pronounced "STOR-gay") is a slow-burning, peaceful, and affectionate love that "just comes naturally" with the passage of time and the enjoyment of shared activities. Storgic relationships lack the ecstatic highs and lows that characterize some other styles; sex occurs late in this type of relationship, and the goals are usually marriage, home, and children. Even if they break up, storgic lovers are likely to remain good friends (Lee, 1973).   *mom & dad ☺*

The storgic lover finds routine home activities relaxing and comfortable. Because there is mutual trust, temporary separations are not a problem. In storgic love, affection develops over the years, as in many lasting marriages. Passion may be replaced by spirituality, respect, and contentment in the enjoyment of each other's company (Murstein, 1974).

(3) Agape   The classical Christian type of love, **agape** (pronounced "AH-gah-pay") is altruistic, self-sacrificing love that is directed toward all humankind. It is a self-giving love in which partners help each other develop their maximum potential without considering their own advantages or costs. Agape is always kind and patient, never jealous or demanding, and does not seek reciprocity. Lee points out, however, that he has not yet found an unqualified example of agape during his interviews.   *biblical*

Intense agape can border on masochism. For example, an agapic person might wait indefinitely for a lover to be released from prison, might tolerate an alcoholic or drug-addicted spouse, or might be willing to live with a partner who engages in illegal activities or infidelity (Lasswell and Lasswell, 1976).   *explains why people stay*

(4) Pragma   According to Lee, **pragma** is rational love based on practical considerations, such as compatibility and perceived benefits. Indeed, it can be described as "love with a shopping list." A pragmatic person seeks compatibility in such things as background, education, religious views, and vocational and professional interests. If one person does not work out, the pragmatic person moves on, quite rationally, to search for someone else.   *– practical*

Pragmatic lovers look out for their partners, encouraging them, for example, to ask for a promotion or to finish college.

spots in margins or blank spaces in the text. The "sticky" notes are a valuable tool for summarizing large quantities of information. They can also be easily removed from the text to use for class discussions, essay writing, or exam review.

5. ONE-SENTENCE SUMMARIES   As you read, stop and reflect after each paragraph or section. Then create a sentence to sum up the information.

As you progress through a passage, you'll gain a deeper understanding of the material while enhancing your retention. If you're a visual learner, you might even consider including quick drawings in your summaries.

E. Skimming and Scanning

The last of our textbook reading strategies is actually two processes: **skimming** and **scanning**. There are different kinds of reading for different situations, even with textbook reading. You need to consider your *purpose* for reading to be able to decide which strategy to use. To get detailed information, using a text-reading strategy like SQ3R works best. But sometimes you don't need detailed information. You might be previewing or reviewing material. Or you might be looking for a specific piece of information. If your purpose is to get a quick overview of the material, or to preview or review, then skimming is the best method. If your purpose is to quickly find a certain fact or piece of information, scanning is the way to go. Neither of these methods requires the reading of every single word in the material, so they also serve as ways to speed up your reading—which is a good thing for college students.

Read the explanations of skimming and scanning that follow. Be sure you understand the distinction between the two—both in the methods themselves, and also the purpose of each. Your instructor will provide you with several practice activities so you can become confident using skimming and scanning, and also confident that you know WHEN to use them.

QUICK TIP

Stop and ask yourself **why** you're reading the material (i.e., your purpose) and then determine which reading strategy is needed.

SKIMMING   Skimming is used to quickly identify the main ideas of a text. When you read the newspaper, you probably don't read from front to back, word for word. Instead you read quickly over the headlines, and maybe the first few sentences of an article to get the main idea and/or to decide if you want to read the entire thing. If not, you continue to move your eyes quickly over the paper, reading the headlines and beginnings of articles. This is very similar to the techniques used in skimming. When you're done reading your newspaper, you have an overview of the news. When you skim an assignment, you have an overview of what it contains when you're done. This is often called a preview or, in SQ3R, the survey.

There are many strategies that can be used for skimming. Here are the most common ones—try them out and decide for yourself which ones work best for you.

How to Skim

- Read the title.
- Read the introduction or first paragraph.
- Read the chapter preview, overview, or highlights.
- Read the first sentence of each or every other paragraph.
- Read headings and subheadings.
- Notice pictures, charts, and graphs.
- Notice bold, italic, or color words/phrases.
- Read the summary or last paragraph.

Now try skimming the Textbook Excerpt for Practice under Heading F to get an overview of the material. Skim it in 30 seconds or less and see if you can fill in the blanks below without looking back at the reading.

Main idea: _____

Who's theories are these? _____

Write any of the theories you remember—how many did you get?

_____

QUICK TIP

Skimming: **WHY?** To get a quick overview. **WHEN?** Before you start reading your assignment. **HOW?** See bulleted steps above.

SCANNING   Scanning is completely different from skimming. You use scanning when you need to quickly locate a specific piece of information. You're using scanning when you look up a number in the telephone book, or a word in the dictionary. When you're skimming, you don't know what you're looking for—you're trying to determine what the reading is about. When you're scanning, you **do** know what you're looking for—a specific piece of information. In scanning you have a question in your mind, and you read a passage only to find the answer, ignoring unrelated information. Scanning involves moving your eyes quickly down the page, seeking specific words, phrases, or numbers.

How to Scan

- State the specific information you're looking for.
- Anticipate how the information will look: Will it have capital letters at the beginning? Will it be a number? Is it one word or several words?

- Use headings and other aids to help you identify sections where your answer is most likely to appear.
- Move your eyes quickly down the page looking for the anticipated type of information.

Scan the following paragraph to find out how many moons Saturn has.

> It's the start of a four-year tour, during which the ship will make at least 76 loops of the planet and engage a dozen cameras and instruments. NASA will be able to tweak the trajectory of the orbiter so it can slalom among nine of Saturn's 31 moons. The grandest of the satellites is Titan, which has long frustrated scientists because its dense atmosphere, laced with organic gases, obscures its surface.
>
> (*Time*, June 28, 2004)

How many moons does Saturn have? Did you find the answer of 31? Were you looking for numerals rather than words? Good job! Now scan the paragraph again to find the answer to this question: How long is the ship's tour supposed to last?

What answer did you find for that question? The correct answer is four years, but the number was written out, and it was hyphenated to the word year, making it harder to find. Remember: If you can't find the answer to your question in the anticipated form, try to think of other ways it might appear. You might also look for another key word in the question, which in this case was the word "tour."

QUICK TIP

Scanning: **WHY?** To find specific information. **WHEN?** Only when you need the answer to a question. **HOW?** See the bulleted steps above.

Skimming and scanning are two easy ways you can improve your reading comprehension, efficiency, and speed. Remember to vary your reading speed and strategies according to your purpose.

QUICK TIP

You don't need to, and shouldn't, read everything in college (or in life) word for word!

F. Textbook Excerpt for Practice

Instructors will find an additional copy of this excerpt in the Instructor's Resource Manual (IRM) so that the pages can be duplicated, if needed, for further practice.

The following textbook excerpt may be used as needed to practice the strategies discussed in this chapter.

Some Theories About Love and Loving

Why and how do we love? Biological explanations tend to focus on why we love. Psychological, sociological, and anthropological approaches try to explain how as well as why.

Lee's Styles of Loving

Canadian sociologist John A. Lee (1973) developed one of the most widely cited and studied approaches to love. Although not a full-fledged theory, Lee's approach was built on his collection of more than 4,000 statements about love from hundreds of works of fiction and nonfiction.

The sources ranged from the literature of ancient Greece (which recognized *agape* and *eros* as two kinds of love), the Bible, and medieval, Victorian, and modern writers. Lee administered a 30-item questionnaire based on this research to people in Canada and Great Britain. From the responses he derived six basic styles of loving: *eros, mania, ludus, storge, agape,* and *pragma* . . . all of which overlap and vary in intensity in real life.

Eros   **Eros** (root of the word *erotic*) is the love of beauty. Because it is also characterized by powerful physical attraction, eros epitomizes "love at first sight." This is the kind of love often described in romance novels, where the lovers are immediately love-struck and experience palpitating hearts, light-headedness, and intense emotional desire.

Erotic lovers want to know everything about the loved one—what she or he dreamed about last night and what happened on the way to work today. Erotic lovers often like to wear matching T-shirts, identical bracelets, and matching colors; to order the same foods when dining out; and to be identified with each other as totally as possible (Lasswell and Lasswell, 1976).

Mania   Characterized by obsessiveness, jealousy, possessiveness, and intense dependency, **mania** may be expressed in anxiety, sleeplessness, loss of appetite, headaches, and even suicide because of real or imagined rejection. Manic lovers are consumed by thoughts of their beloved and have an insatiable need for attention and signs of affection (Lee, 1973). Mania is often associated with low self-esteem and a poor self-concept. As a result, manic people are typically not attractive to those who have a strong self-concept and high self-esteem (Lasswell and Lasswell, 1976).

Ludus   **Ludus** is carefree and casual love that is considered "fun and games." Physical appearance is less important to ludic lovers than self-sufficiency and a nondemanding partner. They try to control their feelings and may have several lovers at one time. They are not possessive or jealous, primarily because they don't want lovers to become dependent on them. Ludic lovers have sex for fun, not emotional rapport. In their sexual encounters they are typically self-centered and may be exploitive because they do not want commitment, which they consider "scary."

Storge   **Storge** (pronounced "STOR-gay") is a slow-burning, peaceful, and affectionate love that "just comes naturally" with the passage of time and the enjoyment of shared activities. Storgic relationships lack the ecstatic highs and lows that characterize some other styles; sex occurs late in this type of relationship, and the goals are usually marriage, home, and children. Even if they break up, storgic lovers are likely to remain good friends (Lee, 1973).

The storgic lover finds routine home activities relaxing and comfortable. Because there is mutual trust, temporary separations are not a problem. In storgic love, affection develops over the years, as in many lasting marriages. Passion may be replaced by spirituality, respect, and contentment in the enjoyment of each other's company (Murstein, 1974).

Agape   The classical Christian type of love, **agape** (pronounced "AH-gah-pay") is altruistic, self-sacrificing love that is directed toward all humankind. It is a self-giving love in which partners help each other develop their maximum potential without considering their own advantages or costs. Agape is always kind and patient, never jealous or demanding, and does not seek reciprocity. Lee points out, however, that he has not yet found an unqualified example of agape during his interviews.

Intense agape can border on masochism. For example, an agapic person might wait indefinitely for a lover to be released from prison, might tolerate an alcoholic or drug-addicted spouse, or might be willing to live with a partner who engages in illegal activities or infidelity (Lasswell and Lasswell, 1976).

Pragma   According to Lee, **pragma** is rational love based on practical considerations, such as compatibility and perceived benefits. Indeed, it can be described as "love with a shopping list." A pragmatic person seeks compatibility in such things as background, education, religious views, and vocational and professional interests. If one person does not work out, the pragmatic person moves on, quite rationally, to search for someone else.

Pragmatic lovers look out for their partners, encouraging them, for example, to ask for a promotion or to finish college. They are also practical in divorce. For example, a couple might stay together until the younger child finishes high school or until both partners find better jobs (Lasswell and Lasswell, 1976).

Chapter Summary

Textbook Strategies: Approximately 70 percent of course information comes from the textbook. It's extremely important to know how to use textbooks and to have strategies for reading them.

Textbook Organizational Aids
- ***Preface***—Author to reader, gives useful information about the book.
- ***Table of Contents***—Like an outline of the book, gives chapter titles, sections, page numbers.
- ***Glossary***—A mini-dictionary of words from the text with meanings as they are used in the text.
- ***Index(es)***—Alphabetical listing of topics in the book with page numbers showing where they can be found. Many textbooks have more than one index.
- ***Appendix(ices)***—Additional information in the back of the book. The text will refer you to the appendices. They're usually lettered A, B, C, and so on.

Textbook Reading Methods
- ***SQ3R***—A five-step method involving surveying, questioning, reading, reciting or highlighting, and reviewing.
- ***5C***—A five-step method using index cards to record key information and vocabulary words and definitions.
- ***Triple Highlighting***—A three-step method using different color highlighters to mark important information as noted by the student, the author, and the instructor.
- ***Reading Graphs, Charts, and Tables***—Read the title, read the labels, determine what type of information is being presented.

Taking Notes While Reading
- ***Cornell Notes***—Main idea on the left side of page, details on the right.
- ***Annotations***—Notes written *directly* in a text or book.
- ***Highlighting***—Featuring information you want to remember in a text or book using highlighters.
- ***"Sticky" Notes***—Placing "sticky" notes (containing key information) directly on book pages for easy removal.
- ***One-Sentence Summaries***—Quick summaries written after reading each paragraph or section.

Skimming and Scanning
- ***Skimming***—Quickly reading over material to get the main idea of the entire reading.
- ***Scanning***—Quickly reading over material to find a specific piece of information.

Check Your Learning (Learning Outcomes)

Have you mastered the Learning Objectives (LOs) for Chapter 3? Place a check mark next to each LO that you're able to do.

_____ LO1—Identify and use textbook organizational aids

_____ LO2—Use three textbook reading methods

_____ LO3—Comprehend information found in graphs, charts, and tables

_____ LO4—Take notes while reading

_____ LO5—Use skimming and scanning

_____ LO6—Use a textbook excerpt to practice textbook strategies

Go back and review the sections that cover any LO you didn't check.

Quick Connections—Chapter Three

NEWS SOURCE CONNECTION

Using a news source (news magazine or newspaper), choose an article that has several headings to read. Apply a text reading method to your news article. Surveying, making questions from the headings, highlighting the answers, and reviewing are also effective strategies to improve your reading of news articles with headings.

TEXTBOOK CONNECTION

Use a textbook from one of your other classes, and if possible, do this activity as you're doing a reading assignment for the other class. Choose either SQ3R, 5C, or triple highlighting, and read your assignment using the chosen textbook reading method. After you've finished, write down at least three things you liked about the method you used, and three things you didn't like. Do the same for each of the other two methods, and then you can determine which method (or perhaps a combination of the methods) works best for you.

NOVEL CONNECTION

The first step of every textbook reading method involves a survey, or preview. Survey or preview the novel you'll read before you start reading. In addition to the sections you preview for a textbook, see what other information is available to preview with your novel (i.e., book jacket). As with a textbook, a novel preview can improve comprehension. It can also help you get into the novel more *quick*ly.

WEB CONNECTION

Conduct a search and find a site on the Internet where you can read about textbook reading methods and possibly find practices. Write a brief description of a textbook reading method that is new to you and seems to be one that would work well. Your instructor may have everyone in the class share the new method each student found. If you find a site with good practice exercises, use them to improve your textbook reading ability.

Four

Critical Reading Strategies

Chapter Preview

LEARNING OBJECTIVES (LOs)

Upon completion of this chapter section, you'll be able to:

- LO1—Make **predictions** based on titles and passages read
- LO2—Make **inferences** based on information implied, but not stated, in passages
- LO3—**Draw conclusions** from information presented in one or more passages

Reading can …
   Take you places you might never go
   and introduce you to people you might
   never know.

LEARNING OBJECTIVES (LOs)

Upon completion of this chapter section, you'll be able to:

■ LO1—Analyze (break down or dissect) and synthesize (arrange or blend) information within a passage in order to:

   • Identify the **writer's purpose**
   • Distinguish between **facts and opinions**
   • Judge the **validity** of a passage
   • Identify **author attitudes**, **bias**, **tone**, and **assumptions**

Strategy Area A: Critical Reading—Predicting, Making Inferences, and Drawing Conclusions

Readiness Quiz A

Match the terms below with the best definitions on the right.

1. _____ critical		**A.** decide, determine
2. _____ imply		**B.** decide from suggestion
3. _____ infer		**C.** forecast or foretell
4. _____ conclude		**D.** evaluative
5. _____ explicit		**E.** suggest
6. _____ predict		**F.** clearly stated

Questions for Discussion

What is critical reading?

How do you read critically?

PART A: CRITICAL READING STRATEGIES OVERVIEW

Predicting, Drawing Conclusions, and Making Inferences

While the word *critical* has various dictionary definitions, when used in the context of critical reading, the term generally involves higher order thinking strategies such as analyzing, comparing, and judging. It is *evaluative* and reflective in nature. As used in the context of this chapter, it refers to any higher order thinking and reading strategies.

   Critical thinking and reading are challenging and complex processes. There are entire courses devoted to these topics. This chapter isn't meant to thoroughly cover this area. It is merely a starting point. **Critical reading** requires consistent practice and continual exposure to a variety of written materials. The practices in this text should be followed up with ongoing practice. Participating in classroom discussions can also be helpful to you as you're exposed to the various perspectives and backgrounds of experience shared among your classmates. Broadening your own background of experience and expanding your perspectives will allow you to read and think more critically.

The first part of this chapter focuses on the critical reading strategies of **predicting**, **making inferences**, and **drawing conclusions**, which require higher level thinking. The latter two strategies often overlap. It's generally necessary to draw a conclusion in order to make an inference. However, not all conclusions require you to make an inference. We'll begin with strategies for predicting.

1. PREDICTING Effective readers are active readers. They begin making predictions about what will come next—right from the beginning of a reading, starting with the title if there is one. Being aware of a writer's pattern of organization (see Chapter 6) may help you to anticipate the direction a reading will take. Test questions sometimes ask the reader to extend (extrapolate or project on the basis of known information) into the future or into a new situation. To make such "predictions," you must first have a clear understanding of the passage. Next, you build upon this information by analyzing the logic used by the writer and/or the sequence of events described. Then, you make choices that are consistent with the passage but that do not *over*extend, or stretch, the ideas expressed there.

QUICK TIP

Notice the way people are described. Use information about their personalities, thoughts, or feelings to determine how they might act or react.

QUICK TIP

After reading and analyzing a passage, ask yourself what might happen as a result of the stated actions or events.

Using the previewing strategy while reading can serve as a major step toward making more accurate predictions. Another great tool involves treating the reading as if it were a two-way conversation. In other words, after each statement a writer makes, the reader can practice an internal dialogue, responding to each point. This strategy simulates what happens in a face-to-face conversation. When you're listening to someone, you generally respond in some way to demonstrate that you've listened and understood. You may ask questions along the way to encourage the speaker to clarify or amplify (expand) what has been said. Active reading, much like active listening, enables you to get much more out of the communication and also to retain it more effectively.

Consider This Title *The Story of an Hour*

When you read this title, what expectations do you have for the information that will follow? You may or may not be accurate, depending upon many factors, but you'll be more prepared for what follows if you at least attempt to anticipate or predict what lies ahead. You would obviously expect some type of story that takes place within an hour. Your internal dialogue might go something like this: "The Story of an Hour . . . hmm, good, that might mean it's not going to be very long. I wonder how someone can make much of a story out of something that only takes an hour. Well, I guess I'll find out."

Don't underestimate the importance of starting to predict by questioning or reflecting upon the title. Sometimes students are in such a hurry that they neglect to pay much attention to the title, or to do a quick preview of the reading. Taking the time to predict can save time later because you get more out of what you read. Continue the active internal dialogue throughout a reading, and you'll be well on your way toward making better predictions.

Now complete a brief practice as you read this short excerpt from Yann Martel's 2001 novel, *Life of Pi*. Pi, the main character in the book, is giving some advice to those who might happen to fall into a lion's pit at a zoo. Try writing short responses where indicated (by the blank lines) within the passage. Then check suggested answers below. To get you started, one possible response for question 1 below might be: "If I fall into a lion's pit? How would that happen? Maybe during a visit to the zoo." Now see if you can come up with your own thoughts and write them on the lines below.

1. So you see, if you fall into a lion's pit,

_____

2. the reason the lion will tear you to pieces

_____

3. isn't because it's hungry—

_____

4. be assured, zoo animals are amply fed—

_____

5. or because it's bloodthirsty,

_____

6. but because you've invaded its territory.

_____

Answers will vary, but the following are some possibilities:

1. Well, I don't intend to ever do that, but if I did, what should I know?
2. Tear me to pieces? Does the lion need a reason? Isn't that just what lions do?
3. Oh, I didn't really think the lion would need to be hungry to tear me to pieces, but what would his reason be, according to you?
4. Yes, I suppose they are, so go on . . .
5. It's not? I guess I thought lions were bloodthirsty. Now you've really got me curious.
6. Oh, yes, I would have invaded its territory. Lions are just protecting their territory then . . . like some people do. Interesting!

2. DRAWING CONCLUSIONS AND MAKING INFERENCES   When what you're reading includes information that isn't clearly or directly stated, it may be necessary for you to **draw a conclusion**. This means that you combine your prior knowledge, or what you already know from past learning or experience, with the new information you're reading to come to a decision.

Here is an example of drawing a **simple conclusion**: John is leaving his home in ten minutes for a meeting that requires him to wear a suit. John owns three suits. However, two of those are at the cleaners. Therefore, you would logically conclude that John will wear the one suit that isn't at the cleaners.

Sometimes, you can draw a conclusion by applying your prior knowledge to stated facts alone. Other times, you'll need to make a judgment based on an idea that is clearly suggested or implied by a writer, although not explicitly stated. This is called an **inference**. When making inferences, keep in mind the main idea and details of a passage. You should be able to defend your inference by first pointing to clearly stated information in a passage, and then reading "between the lines."

Making inferences is a natural part of the thinking process. For instance, if you pass a friend or acquaintance in a hallway and greet that person, but fail to get a response to your greeting, you probably infer something like "she must not have seen me" or "he must be pre-occupied right now" or "gee, she's really stuck up!" The tricky thing about inferences is that, because they are implied, it's possible to be wrong. Perhaps the acquaintance didn't recognize you. Or possibly the friend had just received traumatic news and was too emotional to respond. The more evidence or clues you have to make an accurate inference, the better.

QUICK TIP

Use the "if–then" test to verify your inference. Does it make sense that if **X** (information stated in the passage) is true, then **Y** (your inference) is probably true?

When attempting to draw conclusions (including inferences), be sure you first understand the main idea and details of a passage. Also use context clues, other vocabulary strategies, and a dictionary to clarify any difficult terminology. Keep in mind the sequence of events and/or logical reasoning. Determine what might result from the actions or events the writer has described. Allow your own background of experience or prior knowledge to help you draw a conclusion without reading *too* much into a passage, or *overextending* its content.

QUICK TIP

Draw conclusions that are consistent with the content of the passage by mentally adding your own thoughts or reflections to what you've read. Any inferences you make should be supported by the passage itself in order to be considered logical conclusions.

For example, consider the following passage from the beginning of Dave Pelzer's (1995) autobiographical novel:

SMACK! Mother hits me in the face and I topple to the floor. I know better than to stand there and take the hit. I learned the hard way that she takes that as an act of defiance, which means more hits, or worst of all, no food. I regain my posture and dodge her looks, as she screams into my ears.

A Child Called "It"

What logical inferences can you make regarding the situation described above? The passage doesn't need to tell us directly that this is an ongoing, abusive relationship between a mother and her son. We quickly infer these things. We might also infer that the child is perceptive enough to have learned how best to deal with the abuse. We get a glimpse of the importance of food to this child since "no food" is worse than "more hits." These inferences all fit the context of the passage. We might begin predicting what will follow, but any serious predictions at this point in the book would overextend the information given. As the story unfolds, we can begin to more accurately draw conclusions and make predictions because we have a stronger base of context from which to do this.

DRAWING CONCLUSIONS AND MAKING INFERENCES PRACTICE

Compare two passages which comment on the celebration of Columbus Day. Read both passages and then answer the questions that follow.

Passage 1

There is widespread agreement that Christopher Columbus wasn't the first person to discover America. Many would say that he exhibited cruelty and greed in his treatment of the Native Americans he encountered in the "New World." Columbus opponents submit that these indigenous people were often exploited, oppressed, and enslaved.

The celebration of Columbus Day has been marked by increased controversy in recent years. It is no wonder that enlightened cities have either eliminated the holiday or replaced it with Indigenous Peoples Day.

Passage 2

The politically correct view is that Columbus did not discover America, because people had lived here for thousands of years. Worse yet, it's claimed, the main legacy of Columbus is death and destruction. Columbus is routinely vilified as a symbol of slavery and genocide, and the celebration of his arrival likened to a celebration of Hitler and the Holocaust. The attacks on Columbus are ominous, because the actual target is Western civilization.

Did Columbus "discover" America? Yes—in every important respect. This does not mean that no human eye had been cast on America before Columbus arrived. It does mean that Columbus brought America to the attention of the civilized world, i.e., to the growing, scientific civilizations of Western Europe. The result, ultimately, was the United States of America.

(http://tinyurl.com/o77zw98)

Now answer the following questions:

1. Would you conclude that these two writers agree or disagree?

    _____

2. Which passage would most likely support the celebration of Columbus Day?

    _____

3. List words that enable the reader to "hear" the emotion of the writer in passage 1. In other words, which words may have been used by the writer to trigger an emotional response from the reader? (Example: "exploit" has a negative connotation. Refer to the discussion on connotative language in Chapter 1, Vocabulary Strategies.)

    _____

4. List words that enable the reader to "hear" the emotion of the writer in passage 2.

    _____

Strategy Area B: Critical Reading—Analyzing and Synthesizing

Readiness Quiz B1

Write an **F** before the statements which are facts and an **O** before the statements which are opinions.

1. _____ Jennifer Lopez is beautiful.
2. _____ George Washington was the second president of the United States.
3. _____ College tuition rates in Nebraska are on the rise.
4. _____ Nebraska state taxes are too high.
5. _____ A U.S. president was impeached.
6. _____ Investing in the stock market is risky.

Readiness Quiz B2

Part a: Match the terms below with the correct definitions on the right.

1. _____	valid	**A.**	the act of taking for granted without proof
2. _____	evidence	**B.**	a position or manner indicative of feeling, opinion, or intention toward a person or thing
3. _____	attitude	**C.**	foretell
4. _____	assumption	**D.**	the means of proving or disproving an assertion
5. _____	predict	**E.**	subjective point of view
6. _____	bias	**F.**	well supported by fact

Part b: Choose **T** for true or **F** for false after reading each statement below.

1. _____ A writer's attitude must be either positive or negative.

2. _____ Readers should always refrain from making predictions based upon a reading unless the prediction is stated within the passage.

3. _____ It's possible to recognize unstated ideas a writer accepts as true or takes for granted.

4. _____ A writer may present evidence that is true, but does not actually support his/her argument.

5. _____ The tone of a reading is the underlying feeling the writer creates.

6. _____ It's impossible to determine a writer's purpose unless it is directly stated.

PART B: CRITICAL READING STRATEGIES OVERVIEW

Analyzing and Synthesizing

In addition to predicting, making inferences, and drawing conclusions, readers are often required to *analyze* (break down or dissect) and *synthesize* (arrange or blend) information. It may be necessary to determine a **writer's purpose**, separate **facts** from **opinions**, judge the **validity** of an argument, and/or identify an **author's attitudes**, **bias**, **tone**, and **assumptions**, based on information presented.

1. IDENTIFYING THE WRITER'S PURPOSE   A key element of better comprehension is for the reader to discern the writer's purpose and intended audience. Writers usually have a specific purpose and audience in mind when writing. The purpose will determine how a reading is organized and will also influence the writer's word choices.

Sometimes clues to the writer's purpose will be evident in the title of a reading. Some writers will directly state the purpose. Often, however, the purpose isn't stated, but merely implied. The reader's careful attention to word choices in the titles, headings, and reading will usually pay off in improved understanding of the writer's purpose. And understanding the purpose will greatly enhance the reader's comprehension of the main idea and details of the reading.

Main purposes of a reading may include the following:

- To inform (give facts or clarify)
- To describe (provide word pictures)
- To persuade (change someone's mind and/or behavior)
- To entertain (amuse or provide enjoyment)
- To narrate (tell a story)

It's important to realize, however, that, although a reading usually has one main purpose, the writer may include a variety or mix of minor purposes as well. For a more detailed analysis of some of these (and other) purposes, see Chapter 6, Patterns of Organization Strategies.

WRITER'S PURPOSE PRACTICE

Read the short passages below, and try to determine which of the following is the writer's main purpose: to inform, describe, persuade, entertain, or narrate.

The young woman was tall, with a figure of perfect elegance on a large scale. She had dark and abundant hair, so glossy that it threw off the sunshine with a gleam, and a face which, besides being beautiful from regularity of feature and richness of complexion, had the impressiveness belonging to a marked brow and deep black eyes. She was ladylike, too, after the manner of the feminine gentility of those days . . .

(Hawthorne, 1959)

MAIN PURPOSE: _____

A recent study in the *Journal of Biomechanics* reported that "the neck joint of a common American field ant can withstand pressures up to 5,000 times the ant's weight." Initially, researchers at Ohio State University estimated an ant could withstand pressures reaching just 1,000 times its weight. However, the actual results were much higher. Also, engineers are "studying whether similar joints might enable future robots to mimic the ant's weightlifting ability on earth and in space."

(Adapted from entomologytoday.org 2014)

MAIN PURPOSE: _____

2. FACT AND OPINION   Critical readers need to be able to differentiate between facts and opinions. A fact is an idea that can be proved or disproved. An idea can be a fact even if it is untrue, as long as it can be either proved or disproved (see Readiness Quiz B1, question 2). Opinions usually include words which **interpret** (*explain or show the meaning of*) or **evaluate** (*judge the value of*) something. Sentence number one below is a clear statement of fact; the second sentence reflects an evaluation.

1. The woman who applied for the job had blue eyes and shoulder-length brown hair.
2. A beautiful woman applied for the job.

It's someone's opinion that the woman is beautiful. While there are numerous examples of interpretive words, here are a few more: loving, dangerous, bad, attractive, gentle, improper, brilliant, and finest. Note that all of these words are adjectives, or words used to describe a noun (person, place, or thing).

QUICK TIP

Look for words that **interpret** or **evaluate**. These often indicate an opinion.

Some words clearly indicate that an opinion follows. Examples: *I feel, I think, I believe, in my opinion*. Other words like *possibly, probably, usually, sometimes, often*, or *perhaps* may be used to limit a statement and to allow for the possibility of other viewpoints. Opinions may be valid when properly supported, and *facts* may actually be false.

Some people think that in order for something to be a fact, it must be proven scientifically. The scientific method, however, can only be used to prove repeatable observations. Another method for proving a fact is called legal-historical proof. This kind of proof depends upon exhibits, oral testimony, and written testimony. An example of this type of fact would be that George Washington was the first president of the United States. Such a statement cannot be proved scientifically, yet is a fact based on legal-historical proof.

One other caution when distinguishing between facts and opinions relates to making predictions. Since the future can't be proved by any method, predictions are regarded as opinions.

FACT AND OPINION PRACTICE

Consider the following statements in light of the discussion above. Write **F** for *facts* and **O** for *opinions* and **underline any words that signal evaluation or prediction**:

1. _____   American children watch too much television.

2. _____   Abraham Lincoln was the sixteenth president of the United States.

3. _____   Women are better communicators than men.

4. _____   The state of California will one day fall into the ocean.

5. _____   Mount Rainier in Washington State is 14,410 feet high.

Even experts' opinions may vary. For instance, some doctors promote a high protein, low carbohydrate diet, while other doctors remain skeptical. Some opinions are so widely accepted that they may seem like facts. However, when interpretation or evaluation is involved, statements are generally considered opinions.

The following passage is from an editorial. Identify as many of the interpretive or evaluative words (or phrases) as you can find, and mark or underline them in the passage. Then check the key below it.

> In politics today, there is one constant—a lack of proven, trusted leadership. The array of candidates on both sides is vexing, alarming, and dangerous, not to mention embarrassing. In some cases, the candidates are manifestly unqualified. Each has glaring deficiencies. We need people who are honest, forthright, and intelligent; we need candidates with common-sense ideas founded on our Constitution, history, bedrock beliefs, and values.
>
> *Omaha World Herald* ("Let's Look for New Candidates,"
> April 16, 2016)

Key: The following words and phrases should be marked or underlined: lack of proven, trusted leadership; vexing, alarming, and dangerous; embarrassing; manifestly unqualified; glaring deficiencies; honest, forthright, and intelligent; common-sense ideas; bedrock beliefs; values

3. JUDGING VALIDITY A crucial component of judging the validity of evidence (that is, evidence well supported by facts) is to examine the *source* of the evidence. Determine whether the source represents expertise, research, and/or appropriate data. Next, look at the evidence itself. Evidence that supports a conclusion strengthens an argument, while evidence that contradicts or casts doubt on a conclusion weakens an argument. Review a writer's claim as well as the evidence used to support it.

> ## QUICK TIP
>
> Ask yourself if a new piece of evidence strengthens the writer's claim, weakens the writer's claim, or is irrelevant to the validity (soundness) of the claim.

It's important to determine if a writer has used sound reasoning to develop a logical argument. Do the thoughts flow logically, or are there missing connections between ideas presented? Has the writer been complete in supporting a conclusion? Do any of the writer's claims contradict each other?

How about the author's use of language? Are words chosen to appeal to the reader's emotions rather than his sense of logic? Is the language ambiguous (vague or unclear)?

Another important strategy for judging the validity of an argument is to look for common **fallacies** (false or erroneous ideas) in the reasoning. **While there are at least hundreds of fallacies in logic and they may often overlap, several of the most common are described below. Just as it's essential for a reader to recognize fallacies in an argument, it's important to avoid such fallacies in one's own writing to maintain credibility.**

> *Emotional appeal:* Words, phrases, slogans, or images are used to arouse a favorable response from the reader. Such tactics can be used in advertisements and political campaigns, or in any kind of persuasive writing. Readers need to look beyond the emotional appeal to consider the true validity of the argument.

Examples

A politician uses terms like *freedom* and *the American way* in a persuasive essay. Controversial issues like gay rights and abortion are discussed using positive or negative terms (e.g., *homophobic, pro-life, antichoice*) to sway the reader, apart from the facts. (See discussion on connotative language in Chapter 1, Vocabulary Strategies.)

> ***Attacking the person, or name-calling:*** A person's conclusion is ignored or attacked on the basis of something the person has (or has not) done or said, rather than on the basis of that person's argument. Such fallacies are rampant during political campaigns, but can occur frequently whenever people differ in their perspectives. Attacks on a person and name-calling are used to divert the reader's attention from the real issue.

Examples

Senator X is a left-wing liberal, so why should we listen to anything he has to say?

Mrs. Y claims that teachers aren't doing their jobs, but since she's never been a teacher, how would she know?

> ***Hasty generalization:*** A conclusion is drawn without sufficient evidence or from too small a sample.

Examples

Several police officers in Los Angeles beat up a black man during an arrest. Therefore, the L.A. Police Department is racist.

A pro-life activist shoots and kills an abortionist. Therefore, pro-lifers are dangerous right-wing extremists.

> ***All or nothing:*** Opinions that state or imply the word *all* are generally stereotypes (and similar to hasty generalizations). They often ignore individual differences or relevant data.

Examples

Lawyers are greedy.

All men are insensitive.

Women are more emotional than men.

Children today are spoiled and lazy.

False cause: Many issues are complex. In an attempt to arrive at a conclusion, events are often erroneously linked as having a cause–effect relationship. The fact that one event follows another does not necessitate such a relationship. An outcome may also be the result of multiple causes, not just one.

Examples

No wonder crime is on an upswing; look at all the violence on TV. While violence on TV *may* contribute to the crime rate, the issue is more complicated. Also, it's important to determine if the initial claim—crime is on an upswing—is true before looking at the validity of the causes.

When some children get taller, they get worse grades in school. The lower grades could actually be caused by factors such as increased activities, hormonal issues, higher expectations, or peer pressure.

Testimonial: A famous person endorses a product (or service). People can be swayed by the fame of the person, rather than by the merit of the product.

Examples

Michael Jordan advertises a particular brand of athletic shoes.

Candice Bergen promotes a cellular phone.

FALLACY PRACTICE

Which **fallacy** (i.e., mistake in reasoning) presented in this chapter can you identify for each statement below?

1. Mr. Smith's thoughts on this tax bill don't really matter since he wouldn't be affected by the tax increase.

2. I'm sure a new law which would lower the drinking age would pass because every single one of my friends thinks it's a great idea.

3. There's a high rate of breast cancer in Nebraska. This must be due to the use of pesticides and herbicides which contaminate the drinking water.

4. IDENTIFYING AUTHOR ATTITUDE, BIAS, TONE, AND ASSUMPTIONS
Careful readers will attempt to discern a writer's attitude toward a subject, as well as to *uncover* assumptions a writer has made. The attitude a writer takes toward a subject is often expressed through the use of positive or negative words. (See discussion on connotative language in Chapter 1, Vocabulary Strategies.) A reader's awareness and analysis of word choices will be a major step toward exposing any bias the writer has expressed toward a topic.

When the writer is objective, word choices will often be neutral and/or both sides of an issue will be covered. When the writer expresses his or her own ideas or feelings about a topic, or covers only one side of an issue, the point of view is biased. This type of writing is considered subjective, rather than objective. Besides enabling the reader to pick up on any bias the writer has expressed, word choices used by the writer also help the reader to interpret the tone of the message. The tone may vary throughout a message, and involve an underlying feeling such as humor, anger, or fear.

QUICK TIP

Look for clue words in a passage that signal a writer's attitude toward a subject.

Examples of positive words: enthusiastic, patriotic, sympathetic, admirable, brave, caring, excellent

Examples of negative words: nasty, sarcastic, unfortunate, inadequate, inept, disapproving, substandard

Writers might express, for example, anger, humor, respect, impatience, sympathy, or disapproval. Or they might exhibit a neutral attitude. Pay close attention to word choices.

Opinions often flow from a writer's assumptions. Assumptions are ideas or perspectives that underlie a writer's claim. They sometimes result in stereotypes. Since assumptions are usually unstated and implied, they can be challenging to uncover. Consider the following example:

Orca whales mate for life and travel in family groups.

Science has demonstrated that Orca whales are intelligent.

Therefore, Orca whales should be saved from extinction.

The underlying assumption is that *an animal that displays such human qualities warrants special protection*. Unless the reader agrees with the underlying assumption, the evidence presented may not be valid for that reader.

QUICK TIP

Sometimes, you might identify a **missing** piece in the writer's logic that helps uncover an assumption.

Picking up on an author's attitudes and assumptions usually requires the reader to make inferences and draw conclusions (see the beginning of the chapter). Consider the following statement from a passage comparing human and animal cultures:

> Our culture lets us make up for having lost our strength, claws, long teeth, and other defenses.

What assumption has the writer made?

The underlying assumption is that *humans evolved from animals*. If the reader agrees with this assumption, it may be more difficult to uncover the assumption. However, for a reader who does not accept the theory of evolution, such a statement may stand out and cause the reader to question the validity of the argument.

Writing Like a Reader

How does a good debater prepare for a debate? The process involves gathering not only information which supports the debater's stance on a topic, but also gathering information for the opposing point of view. When an audience sees that the debater has considered all of the facts, not only those that support his or her position, they will trust the debater more. When preparing to write persuasively, a critical thinker will take a similar approach.

A related factor in the writing process is modifying one's tone according to the intended audience. If you enjoy rap music and read a passage that takes an overtly negative tone toward rap, chances are that you wouldn't be very receptive to the author's argument. Likewise, when you write, you should consider your own audience's attitude toward the topic. You don't want to adopt a tone that will alienate your audience. Notice that the more neutral tone of the second paragraph below might be more well-received by a group of public high school students than the first.

> *I'm disgusted by rap music, and you should be too. It's the devil's music. If you listen to it, you are just as guilty as the ones who write and produce it. The twisted and mindless lyrics should repulse any thinking human being. I hope you will join me in a boycott of such perversion.*

> *While rap music is both prevalent and popular in today's culture, its effects have become a matter of controversy. Although some critics claim that rap has contributed to teen pregnancy and unprotected sexual activity, others view it as an art form not so different from poetry.*

ATTITUDE, BIAS, TONE, AND ASSUMPTION PRACTICE

The following is a paragraph from the 1960 novel, *Night,* by Elie Wiesel. Wiesel is struggling with his faith in God as a result of his experience in concentration camps during the Holocaust. These are his thoughts.

"Blessed be the Name of the Eternal!"

Why, but why should I bless Him? In every fiber I rebelled. Because He had had thousands of children burned in His pits? Because He kept six crematories working night and day, on Sundays and feast days? Because in His great might He had created Auschwitz, Birkenau, Buna, and so many factories of death? How could I say to Him: "Blessed art Thou, Eternal, Master of the Universe, Who chose us from among the races to be tortured day and night, to see our fathers, our mothers, our brothers, end in the crematory? Praised be Thy Holy Name, Thou Who hast chosen us to be butchered on Thine altar?"

1. What assumptions is Wiesel making in this passage?

_____

_____

_____

_____

2. How would you describe Wiesel's attitude toward God in the passage above? What words or phrases used in the paragraph support your response?

_____

_____

_____

_____

3. What other words might you use to describe the overall tone of this passage?

_____

4. Is Wiesel expressing a biased or a neutral point of view?

_____

Chapter Summary

Critical Thinking: Generally involves higher order thinking skills such as analyzing, comparing, and judging. It is *evaluative* and reflective in nature. As used in the context of this chapter, it refers to any higher order thinking and reading skills.

Predicting: Previewing a reading, beginning with the title, is a major step toward making more accurate predictions. Notice the way people are described, and after reading and analyzing a passage, ask yourself what might happen as a result of the stated actions or events.

Making Inferences: An idea that is clearly *suggested* or *implied* by a writer, although not *explicitly* stated. When making inferences, keep in mind the main idea and details of a passage. Use the if–then test to verify inferences.

Drawing Conclusions: It's generally necessary to draw a conclusion in order to make an inference. However, not all conclusions require you to make an inference. Determine a consequence that is consistent with the content of the passage by mentally adding your response to the end of the reading and asking if it fits logically.

Analyzing and Synthesizing: Readers are often required to analyze (break down or dissect) and synthesize (arrange or blend) information.

Writer's Purpose: Writers usually have a specific purpose and audience in mind, which often determines the organizational pattern and word choices used. Main purposes of a reading may be to **inform**, to **describe**, to **persuade**, to **entertain**, or to **narrate**.

Fact and Opinion: A fact is an idea that can be proved or disproved. An idea can be a fact even if it is untrue, as long as it can be either proved or disproved. Opinions usually include words which **interpret** (*explain or show the meaning of*) or **evaluate** (*judge the value of*) something.

Judging Validity: First determine whether the source represents expertise, research, and/or appropriate data. Then decide whether the **evidence** strengthens the writer's claim, weakens the writer's claim, or is irrelevant to the validity of the claim. Make sure that arguments used flow logically and avoid contradictions. Look for common **fallacies** such as emotional appeals and all-or-nothing thinking.

Identifying Author Attitude, Bias, Tone, and Assumptions: Look for **clue words** in a passage that signal a writer's attitude toward a subject. Begin with titles and headings. Be on the lookout for assumptions (ideas or perspectives that underlie a writer's claim). These are often challenging to uncover because they tend to be unstated or implied.

Check Your Learning (Learning Outcomes)

Have you mastered the Learning Objectives (LOs) for Chapter 4? Place a check mark next to each LO that you're able to do.

PART A

_____ LO1—Make predictions based on titles and passages read

_____ LO2—Make inferences based on information implied, but not stated, in passages

_____ LO3—Draw conclusions from information presented in one or more passages

PART B

_____ LO1—Analyze (break down or dissect) and synthesize (arrange or blend) information within a passage in order to:

- _____ Identify the writer's purpose
- _____ Distinguish between facts and opinions
- _____ Judge the validity of a passage
- _____ Identify author attitudes, bias, tone, and assumptions

Go back and review the sections that cover any LO you didn't check.

Quick Connections—Chapter Four

NEWS SOURCE CONNECTION

Using a news source (news magazine or newspaper), choose a persuasive article or an editorial to read. Find and mark (or list) two to three conclusions or claims the writer has made. Then try to identify supporting evidence the

writer has used, and evaluate the validity of the claims. Also attempt to identify any assumptions the writer has made.

TEXTBOOK CONNECTION

Use a textbook from one of your other classes, and if possible, do this activity
as you're completing a reading assignment for the other class. Choose a section of the text you haven't yet read, and write the heading for that section on
a sheet of paper. Based solely on that heading, identify two or more questions
you expect the following section of text to answer. Then continue reading to
find out if your *predictions* were accurate.

NOVEL CONNECTION

After reading at least one chapter of a novel, identify two main characters.
Draw conclusions about these characters, and list four or five character traits
for each. (Examples might include words like *humorous, outgoing, stubborn,
angry,* and *loving.*) For each trait listed, identify a line or passage in the chapter that supports your conclusions.

WEB CONNECTION

Go to a news source website, such as the *Newsweek* or the *New York Times*
site. Choose an article that looks interesting, and skim it to make sure it
includes both facts and opinions. List three statements of fact and three statements of opinion that you found (or print the article and highlight or mark
them).

Five

Figurative Language Strategies

Chapter Preview

Figurative Language Strategies Overview
A. Metaphor and Simile
B. Personification
C. Hyperbole
D. Others: Analogy, Irony, Understatement, Idioms

LEARNING OBJECTIVES (LOs)

Upon completion of this chapter, you'll be able to:

- LO1—Recognize and interpret *metaphors* and *similes* in written context, and differentiate between them
- LO2—Recognize and interpret *personification* in written context
- LO3—Recognize and interpret *hyperbole* in written context
- LO4—Recognize analogy, irony, understatement, and idioms

True Story . . .
A mother asked her young son to "keep an eye on" his baby brother. The son looked confused and asked, "but mommy, how do I take it out?"

Readiness Quiz A

Match the terms below with the correct definitions on the right.

1. _____ simile	**A.** human qualities attributed to an object, animal, or idea
2. _____ metaphor	**B.** a deliberate overstatement or exaggeration
3. _____ personification	**C.** using *like* or *as* to make a comparison between two things
4. _____ hyperbole	**D.** symbolical, not literal
5. _____ figurative	**E.** making a comparison between two things without using *like* or *as*

Readiness Quiz B

Now match the terms below with the correct examples on the right.

1. _____ simile	**A.** The tulips danced in the breeze.
2. _____ metaphor	**B.** She's as lovely as a bright spring day.
3. _____ personification	**C.** He's at least a thousand years old.
4. _____ hyperbole	**D.** We peered out upon a fluffy, white blanket of snow.

FIGURATIVE LANGUAGE STRATEGIES OVERVIEW

This chapter focuses on four common types of figurative language: **simile**, **metaphor**, **personification**, and **hyperbole**. Four additional types of figurative language are defined and briefly explained near the end of this chapter. Figurative language is frequently used in poetry and other types of literature, but may show up in any kind of writing. It can greatly enhance the imaginative element of the reading process and, therefore, create some challenges in interpretation. At the same time, figurative language can assist the reader in understanding and making connections between the writer's thoughts and the reader's world of experience. Figurative language often invokes imagination rather than literal interpretation. Recognizing and understanding common forms of figurative language improves the reader's ability to make appropriate interpretations and applications of the language. You may rarely need to identify the actual figurative language terms, so focus on recognizing these common figures of speech and allowing them to help you draw connections the writer is implying.

QUICK TIP

When you recognize a writer's use of figurative language, attempt to create pictures in your mind of images the writer is "painting" for the reader. This is a form of visualization.

A. Metaphor and Simile

In one line of a poem entitled "We Are a People," the writer mentions a "moccasin path." When readers see the word "moccasin," a picture may take shape in their minds, triggering an association with a specific group of people, Native Americans. Being able to create such mental pictures and form such associations will enable readers to more accurately interpret the other lines of the poem. In some writings, one picture like this may be the foundation for understanding the entire piece. In the poem "We Are a People," the people group is never identified . . . except through the use of implied metaphors and images. Be sure to pay careful attention to titles and headings, where clue words often show up.

QUICK TIP

Sometimes, one word or phrase may be the foundation for understanding an entire reading. Clue words often show up in titles or headings.

In an essay titled *The Attic of the Brain,* Lewis Thomas helps the reader create a mental picture of an attic in an old house and then begins to describe how the brain has its own kind of "attic." An astute reader will begin to create her own images simply by reading a few words presented in an intriguing title. The brain does not have a physical "attic," but the **metaphor** enables the reader to draw relevant and enlightening comparisons. Such comparisons are sometimes signaled by such clue words as *like, as,* or *similar* to introduce a simile. For example, Thomas makes the following two direct comparisons, or **similes**, toward the end of his passage:

> Attempting to operate one's own mind, powered by such a magical instrument as the human brain, strikes me as rather like using the world's biggest computer to add columns of figures, or towing a Rolls-Royce with a nylon rope.

Here the human brain is compared to a magical instrument, and "attempting to operate" one's mind is compared to two other unlikely tasks.

Since **similes** are usually easier to recognize than **metaphors**, let's practice a few of those.

> A quarrelsome wife is like a constant dripping on a rainy day.
>
> (*Proverbs* 27:15)

What two things are being compared here? A quarrelsome wife and a constant dripping of rain. The writer is attempting to communicate some things about a quarrelsome wife using constant dripping as the "picture." What do you think of when you picture a constant dripping? While some people might actually enjoy the sound of rain, we know from the writer's choice of the word *quarrelsome* that he is creating a negative comparison. Use of the word *constant* implies something that might be repeated to the point of irritation. The reader may identify constant dripping as being tiresome, annoying, or even exasperating—not a glowing comparison for a quarrelsome wife.

Here's another **simile**:

> Like clouds and wind without rain is a man who boasts of his gifts falsely.
>
> (*Proverbs* 25:14)

In this verse, the gifts of a man who boasts falsely are compared to clouds and wind without rain. Since clouds and wind often result in rain, the picture of clouds and wind *without* rain helps the reader understand that a braggart's gifts may not live up to what is expected.

Now look at one more **simile**:

> Some people view the commitment of marriage as an alligator from some murky swamp.
>
> (Albom, 1997)

In this sentence, the commitment of marriage is compared to an alligator from a murky swamp. Let's first think of the pictures the word *alligator* calls up. Alligators might be seen as frightening and dangerous. In addition, a murky swamp could be described as dark or gloomy—a place you wouldn't want to enter. The reader gets the impression that some people see the commitment of marriage as something frightening, dangerous, and forbidding. Just as a murky swamp makes it hard to see what's ahead, it might be difficult for some to commit to a relationship when what will happen in the future is impossible to predict.

Here's one more sentence which includes both a **simile** and a **metaphor**:

> ALS* is like a lit candle; it melts your nerves and leaves your body a pile of wax.
>
> (Albom, 1997)

1. What is the simile? <u>ALS is like a lit candle</u>

2. What is the metaphor? <u>your body a pile of wax</u>

SIMILE/METAPHOR PRACTICE ONE

The practice exercise below is taken from the following website:

http://volweb.utk.edu/Schools/bedford/harrisms/1poe.htm

First identify each sentence as a **simile** (S), or a **metaphor** (M), by writing the appropriate letter in the blank preceding each number. Remember that a **simile** is using words such as *like* or *as* to make a comparison between two things, while a **metaphor** makes a comparison between two things without using *like* or *as*.

_____   1. The baby was like an octopus, grabbing at all the cans on the grocery store shelves.

_____   2. As the teacher entered the room she muttered under her breath, "This class is like a three-ring circus!"

_____   3. The giant's steps were thunder as he ran toward Jack.

_____   4. The pillow was a cloud when I put my head upon it after a long day.

_____   5. I feel like a limp dishrag.

_____   6. Those girls are like two peas in a pod.

_____   7. The fluorescent light was the sun during our test.

_____   8. No one invites Harold to parties because he's a wet blanket.

---

*ALS, or amyotrophic lateral sclerosis, is a disease of the nerve cells in the brain and spinal cord that control voluntary muscle movement. ALS is also known as Lou Gehrig's disease. (http://www.ninds.nih.gov/disorders/amyotrophiclateralsclerosis/detail_ALS.htm)

_____   **9.** The bar of soap was a slippery eel during the dog's bath.

_____   **10.** Ted was as nervous as a cat with a long tail in a room full of rocking chairs.

Now go back through the 10 sentences above, and in the blanks below, identify the two items being compared. The first one is done for you.

1. baby	octopus
2.	
3.	
4.	
5.	
6.	
7.	
8.	
9.	
10.	

SIMILE/METAPHOR PRACTICE TWO

The next practice on **similes** and **metaphors** lists expressions used in the novel *Tuesdays with Morrie* by Mitch Albom. Identify each thought as a **simile** (S), or a **metaphor** (M), in the blanks below:

_____   **1.** The newspaper had been *my lifeline, my oxygen.*

_____   **2.** He had created a *cocoon* of human activities—conversation, interaction, affection . . .

_____   **3.** . . . and it filled his life like an *overflowing soup bowl.*

_____   **4.** Morrie had become a *prisoner of his chair.*

_____   **5.** Sometimes he would close his eyes and try to draw the air up into his mouth and nostrils, and it seemed as if he were *trying to lift an anchor.*

Now reread each thought above, and try to rewrite each italicized word or phrase in a more literal way on the lines below. The first one is done for you.

A. <u>something needed to live or to stay alive</u>

B. _____

C. _____

D. _____

E. _____

SIMILE/METAPHOR PRACTICE THREE

The final practice on **metaphors** is a more challenging reading in which **metaphors** are implied, though not directly stated. Read the following poem and then answer the questions that follow.

Of One Self-Slain

By Charles Hanson Towne

When he went blundering back to God,
His songs half written, his work half done,
Who knows what paths his bruised feet trod,
What hills of peace or pain he won?
I hope God smiled and took his hand,
And said, "Poor truant, passionate fool!
Life's book is hard to understand:
Why couldst thou not remain at school?"

Some students understand the main point of this poem immediately, while others struggle. It's often a good idea to begin to bring meaning to a reading by starting with the title.

1. What do the title and the first line of the poem suggest about the person in the poem?

   _____

   _____

2. What might "bruised feet" in line 3 represent?

   _____

   _____

3. List at least three more **metaphors** from the poem and what each represents:

   _____

   _____

   _____

   _____

   _____

   _____

4. How would you describe the **tone** of the poem?

_____

B. Personification

Personification is a writing technique that attributes human qualities to an object, animal, or idea. While this technique is often used in poetry and other forms of creative writing, it is also commonly used in other types of writing. Underlined in the sentences below are some simple examples of personification:

> The <u>candle flame danced wildly</u> when the door blew open.
>
> Her <u>heart jumped for joy</u> when her missing child entered the room.
>
> The <u>thermostat</u> was set so high, it <u>baked the air</u> in the small house.
>
> The <u>falling leaves warned</u> us of the changing season.
>
> The <u>moon made its nightly climb</u> over the fading horizon.

When **personification** is used, it may bring life and meaning to a description—much like a picture or video may "breathe life" (another example of personification) into the words on a page. The technique helps us, the readers, to form our own mental pictures based on prior knowledge or past experiences. Consider this line from poet Kahlil Gibran (1923):

> But let there be spaces in your togetherness,
>
> And let the winds of the heavens dance between you.

The first half of the thought is literal and clear, while the second half is poetic and helps us to "see" the truth of the literal half.

QUICK TIP

As with other forms of figurative language, **personification** often helps the reader to form mental pictures based on prior knowledge or past experiences.

Now read the following passage from _20/20 Hindsight_, an essay by Jay Ford (1996), and answer the questions that follow.

> In Kenya I felt more free than I have ever felt before. The only thing holding me captive was the earth which would grow the

food, the sky which would quench the earth of its thirst, and the sun which would warm and help all things to grow. But these masters were sure to give back all that you have put in.

What three objects were holding the writer *captive*?

1. Earth
2. Sky
3. Sun

What are your thoughts on how these objects might hold someone captive, and why does the writer call them *masters*?

Though answers may vary, you might have considered the need for these aspects of nature in order for one to live.

PERSONIFICATION PRACTICE

Underline each specific example of **personification** below and then identify its meanings in your own words on the lines that follow.

From our cabin window, we stared at the rays of sunlight dancing on the surface of the pond.

_____

_____

_____

_____

In truth, I felt as if my life was stranded out on the high dive, about to leap into unknown waters. (Kidd, 2002)

_____

_____

_____

_____

Ornately carved, the massive doors of the Notre Dame lie open, arms receiving the weary and I am that. (Voskamp, 2010)

_____

_____

_____

_____

C. Hyperbole

A **hyperbole** (pronounced hy-peī-bò-lē) is a deliberate overstatement or exaggeration.

Examples of Common Types of Hyperbole

He was *scared to death*.

Don't go out without a coat; you'll *catch your death* (of cold).

I'm so hungry, *I could eat a horse*.

We're *starving*!

I've told you *a thousand times* to pick up those toys!

I thought that sermon would last *forever*!

In the 1982 book *And More by Andy Rooney*, humorist Andrew A. Rooney includes a chapter entitled "Living Is Dangerous to Your Health." The title and chapter are both exaggerations meant to make fun of the constant bombardment of news indicating how many things are bad for us. **Hyperbole** is often used to provide humor or special effect. The overstatement makes an impression on the reader.

QUICK TIP

As with other forms of figurative language, **hyperbole** isn't meant to be taken literally. The overstatement or exaggeration is used to make an impression on the reader. It may provide humor or some other special effect. Ask yourself what effect the writer may be trying to produce.

You may have seen or heard the common phrase "blazing inferno." According to writer and lexicographer Betty Kirkpatrick (*Clichés*, 1996), the phrase is used often by journalists in headlines such as "man leaps from roof in blazing inferno." Kirkpatrick asserts that the term would "properly be used to describe a very large and dangerous fire, but is in fact often used to describe anything bigger than a small garden rubbish fire, the tabloid press having a weakness for exaggeration, which sells more copies of newspapers."

Another well-known hyperbole is included in the following stanza from Ralph Waldo Emerson's *Concord Hymn*, written for the dedication of the Obelisk, a battle monument commemorating the valiant efforts put forth by citizens of Concord, Massachusetts on April 19, 1775. The event described marked the start of the Revolutionary War.

> *By the rude bridge that arched the flood,*
> *Their flag to April's breeze unfurled;*
> *Here once the embattled farmers stood;*
> *And <u>fired the shot heard round the world.</u>*

Given that a shot couldn't be heard *round the world*, how would you interpret the **hyperbole** underlined in the above stanza?

_____

_____

_____

_____

Did your answer include the idea that the shot had far-reaching consequences or interest? If so, you're on the right track! Great!

Hyperbole Practice

Now write a more literal alternative for each of the **hyberboles** in italics below:

1. He made *a ton of money* in the stock market.

   _____

2. He has *a million relatives.*

   _____

3. *Her beauty could launch a thousand ships.*

   _____

4. *She is a giant in this industry.*

   _____

5. *His mouth could rival the Grand Canyon.* I can never get a word in when "we" talk.

   _____

D. Others: Analogy, Irony, Understatement, and Idioms

While this chapter focused on four common types of figurative language, there are many more types.

Four additional forms of figurative language frequently encountered include **analogy**, **irony**, **understatement**, and **idioms**.

Analogy

Definition: Finding likeness in two or more things that are seemingly dissimilar

Note that analogies are similar to metaphors and similes. However, analogies are a bit more complex. Analogies help to explain the similarities in the relationship between two things, while metaphors and similes tend to replace the meaning of a word with another word or phrase.

Example: "The universe is like a safe to which there is a combination. But the combination is locked up in the safe." (DeVries, 1965)

Irony

Definition: Using words to suggest the opposite of what the words literally mean or the opposite of what might be expected

Examples: A fish drowns; An attempt is made to ban a book, but due to the negative attention given to the book, more people read it.

Understatement

Definition: Using words that are purposely restrained or limited for effect

Example: "Not bad, eh?" (after a baseball player hits two consecutive home runs)

Idioms

Definition: A phrase of two or more words understood to mean something quite different from what the words would typically imply

Idioms can be a special challenge for English language learners because the meaning of a group of words as a unit differs from the meanings of the words used separately. See the examples below. However, many more idioms and their meanings are available online. Search for "idioms" on Google, Bing, Yahoo, or another search engine.

Common Examples:

Idiom: "Don't cry over spilt milk."
Meaning: Don't complain about something that happened in the past.

Idiom: Something costs "an arm and a leg."
Meaning: Something is quite expensive.

Idiom: "Every cloud has a silver lining."
Meaning: Good things can come from difficulties or challenges.

"Idiom: We don't often "see eye to eye."
Meaning: We don't often agree on things.

Writing Like a Reader

While writing, attempt to "flavor" your thoughts with figurative language and descriptive words, if appropriate. Besides adding interest, the use of figurative and descriptive language creates mental images that "paint" pictures for readers and trigger their imaginations. Instead of merely *telling* readers about something, *show* them. The first paragraph below *tells* the thoughts of an expectant mother while the second paragraph *shows* those thoughts.

As I felt those first signs of life inside of me, I felt happier than I'd ever felt before. I prepared your room months before you even came home from the hospital. I cleaned and decorated just for you.

As I felt those first flutters of life, signs of the precious gift growing inside me, my heart nearly exploded in anticipation. Months before my due date, a small, sun-lit bedroom sparkled and anxiously awaited your arrival. The bright walls and soft furnishings whispered a welcoming lullaby.

Chapter Summary

Figurative Language: Frequently used in poetry and other types of literature, but may show up in any kind of writing. It isn't to be taken literally, but is used to add interest and stimulate the imagination. While knowing the specific terms for common forms of figurative language may not be necessary, the reader's awareness and recognition of these forms should help create mental pictures that bring meaning and depth to a reading.

Metaphor: Draws comparisons between two things without using words such as *like, as,* or *similar.* These also help the reader to see how things are alike but may be more challenging to recognize or interpret than similes, since the comparison word clues aren't directly stated.

Simile: Draws comparisons between two things, using words such as *like, as,* or *similar.* These help the reader to see how things are alike. One word or phrase may sometimes provide the foundation for understanding an entire reading. Pay special attention to titles and headings.

Personification: Attributes human qualities to an object, animal, or idea. As with other types of figurative language, personification may bring life and meaning to a description and help readers to form mental pictures based on prior knowledge or past experiences.

Hyperbole: A deliberate overstatement or exaggeration. As with other forms of figurative language, hyperbole isn't meant to be taken literally. The exaggeration is used to make an impression on the reader. It may provide humor or some other special effect. Ask yourself what effect the writer may be trying to produce.

Check Your Learning (Learning Outcomes)

Have you mastered the Learning Objectives (LOs) for Chapter 5? Place a check mark next to each LO that you're able to do.

_____ LO1—Recognize and interpret ***metaphors*** and ***similes*** in written context, and differentiate between them

_____ LO2—Recognize and interpret ***personification*** in written context

_____ LO3—Recognize and interpret ***hyperbole*** in written context

_____ LO4 Recognize analogy, irony, understatement, and idioms

Go back and review the sections that cover any LO you didn't check.

Quick Connections—Chapter Five

NEWS SOURCE CONNECTION

Using a news source (news magazine or newspaper), skim the source, looking for examples of the four types of figurative language covered in this chapter. Find and mark (or list) at least two examples of each. Then identify how each example could be stated in a literal way.

TEXTBOOK CONNECTION

Some textbooks lend themselves more to locating figurative language than others. If you're reading a textbook for another course, and the text does incorporate figurative language, write the title of the text and then list at least four figurative expressions you're able to find. Also write a short response, explaining why that subject area might lend itself to expressions of figurative language. If you have a textbook for another course that does not incorporate figurative language, write a brief response explaining why literal language is more appropriate for that text. Then list at least five general courses that probably would use textbooks which incorporate figurative language.

NOVEL CONNECTION

Using a course novel, or any novel acceptable to your instructor, skim for examples of the four types of figurative language covered in this chapter. Try to find at least two examples of each. Then prepare a matching game for another student in the course by folding a clean sheet of paper into eighths and writing one example (you've found) on each section. On a separate sheet of paper, also folded into eight sections, restate each example in a literal way. Number each section on both sheets so that the matches have the same numbers. Then cut each sheet, clipping all the figurative expressions together and all the literal restatements together. You'll have two separate piles. Be sure they are scrambled, so that they are ready to be matched by another student.

WEB CONNECTION

Using Google or another search engine, type *figurative language* in the search bar. Find sites that end with *.edu* and that are also connected with a university or college. Search until you find at least four types of figurative language that aren't included in this chapter. List the four types you found, and at least one example of each. At the bottom of your paper, be sure to identify the sites you used as well.

Six

Patterns of Organization Strategies

Chapter Preview

Patterns of Organization Strategies Overview

A. Narration (Time Order)
B. Description
C. Process Analysis
D. Classification
E. Comparison/Contrast
F. Cause and Effect

LEARNING OBJECTIVES (LOs)

Upon completion of this chapter, you'll be able to:

- LO1—Recognize different patterns of organization
- LO2—Identify the organization within each pattern
- LO3—Analyze information from each pattern
- LO4—Understand the purpose of each pattern

A writer uses patterns to organize writing; a reader must use them to organize reading.

Readiness Quiz

Section 1: Match the following terms on the left with the definitions on the right:

1. _____ Narration (Time Order)   **A.** to explain parts, or to sort into categories

2. _____ Cause and Effect   **B.** to relate an event or a series of events

3. _____ Process Analysis   **C.** to define a term or clarify the meaning

4. _____ Classification   **D.** to explain how to do something

5. _____ Comparison/Contrast   **E.** shows the relationships between two or more events

6. _____ Definition and Example   **F.** to show how things are alike and different

Section 2: Match the following statements on the left with the terms on the right:

1. _____ The first thing you need to do to organize your closet is to get some shelves. Second, you need some boxes and pens for labeling.   **A.** Cause and Effect

2. _____ Feng shui is the ancient Chinese art of harmony and balance.   **B.** Narration (Time Order)

3. _____ I can't wait to tell you about the father-daughter dance at my wedding!   **C.** Classification

4. _____ Movies have various genres such as horror, comedy, romance, or drama.   **D.** Comparison/Contrast

5. _____ Because my father is in prison, I am raising my brothers and sisters.   **E.** Definition and Example

6. _____ Country music and rock 'n' roll are alike in some ways, but they can be very different.   **F.** Process Analysis

PATTERNS OF ORGANIZATION STRATEGIES OVERVIEW

Why does a reader need to understand the author's pattern of organization? A pattern of organization refers to how a paragraph's sentences are structured or arranged. Understanding how to recognize the different patterns improves your reading comprehension. When authors write, they choose a structure or style that fits the topic. As readers begin to recognize the various patterns, relationships among ideas become clearer. This clarity improves comprehension because the reader is better able to follow the development of an idea from start to finish. When reading, look for the controlling idea, a word or thought that is repeated within the passage. The sentences of a paragraph are said to be *united* when they work together to support the main idea.

Readers should ask the following questions when reading:

1. How are the author's details organized? Is he or she telling a story, describing something, showing a process?
2. What unifies or ties together the author's writing? Are key words or ideas repeated, and/or are transitional words used?

Writers often mix patterns in their writings. This approach provides the reader with various ways to understand the subject. For example, the subject may first be described and then a story may follow. Being aware of these patterns enables the reader to make more connections among the details and improves comprehension.

This chapter addresses the following six patterns of organization:

1. Narration (Time Order)
2. Cause and Effect
3. Process Analysis
4. Classification
5. Comparison/Contrast
6. Definition and Example

Purpose of Organizational Patterns

Pattern	Purpose
Narration (Time Order)	To relate an event or series of events leading to an outcome
Cause and Effect	To show relationships between two or more events
Process Analysis	To explain how to do something or how something occurs
Classification	To explain parts of a whole or to sort into categories or groups
Comparison/Contrast	To tell how two things are similar or different, or both
Definition and Example	To define a term, either to clarify its meaning or to suggest a new meaning

Important Aspects of Each Organizational Pattern

Pattern	Important Aspects
Narration (Time Order)	Story, told in first or third person; tells who, what, why, when, where, and how; sequence of events is important. **Transition words (after, later, during, never, suddenly, last)**
Cause and Effect	Shows how one event created a new event; shows effects of a cause; shows the causes of an effect. **Transition words (because, since, cause, as a result, effect, outcome)**
Process Analysis	Describes a method of doing something; sequence is extremely important; look for steps and order. **Transition words (first, next, after, before, following, stage, secondly)**
Classification	Divides a subject into various parts or identifies a member of a group based on similar characteristics; look for part-to-whole relationship or various categories into which a large number of things can be sorted. **Transition words (part, type, group, category, class, member)**
Comparison/Contrast	Shows how two things are alike or different. Can be organized subject by subject, or point by point. **Transition words (in comparison, similarly, like, in contrast, on the other hand, whereas)**
Definition and Example	Defines a person, place, thing, or idea by explaining the characteristics that distinguish it from others in its class. **Transition words (for example, to illustrate, such as, means, is defined, can be seen as)**

Transition Words

Transitions or **signal words** are words or phrases that allow the reader to follow a writer's ideas. They assist in *bridging* or connecting the ideas in a passage and create a sense of unity. To learn more about important transitions that can help you verify the pattern of organization the author has chosen, refer to the previous charts. The charts above contain a list of common transitions or signals for each pattern of organization. The charts also summarize the purposes and important aspects of each pattern to aid in identification of the pattern.

QUICK TIP

Transition words create a powerful link between ideas in a writing.
Think of them as a bridge.

The best way to learn to recognize patterns of organization is by reading and practicing. The following pages provide examples of each of the patterns. Read the examples and answer the questions that follow. Make sure you do not skip the Preparing to Read introductions, which will guide your understanding of each pattern.

A. Narration (Time Order)

PREPARING TO READ Can you recall special memories from your childhood? You know the memories that seem to stand out from the others? Maybe it was nothing spectacular, but just warm memories that still make you smile. Chic Mancuso is sharing his memories of what a day was like with his grandfather who was an Italian immigrant. As you read, notice it is a retelling of a specific event. Notice the relevance in the sequence of events in understanding the progression or how one thing leads to another. Look for transition words that help the reader follow the sequence of events.

THINGS I REMEMBER GROWING UP

From the Memoirs of Joseph (Chic) Mancuso

I remember in 1935 when I was 10 going with my grandfather (my mother's father) to the city market. At the back of his house on South 11th Street, he had a barn. He had a wagon that he hitched to the horse in the barn. Before the weather got cold in early spring, he would go to the city market around 5:00 a.m. to buy fruits and vegetables. He bought so much it filled the back of his wagon! He would then take the wagon filled with fruits and vegetables through the alleys on the route where he sold the produce to his customers. It was a treat for me to go with him when school got out in mid-June. I would sleep over at their house, and we would get up at about 4:00 a.m. We would have a great big breakfast before we headed to 11th and Jackson, the location of the city market, to buy fruits and vegetables. We rode into the alleys selling our produce around 7:30 a.m. My grandfather worked until all the fruits and vegetables were sold, usually around 3:30 p.m. If he had a few things left that wouldn't spoil, he would save them to sell the next day. It always amazed me that we would ride in the wagon all of that time and neither of us ever said a word! He couldn't speak any English, and I couldn't speak any Italian. Also, I still don't know how the customers knew how much the fruits and vegetables cost, how he was able to make change, and how he made a living doing that job. Once we got home, his wife and daughters would help him put the wagon in the barn and take care of the horse. He would immediately go sit in his rocking chair in the living room. One aunt would have his pipe filled and lit for him. Another aunt would bring him something to drink, and Nana would take off his shoes and rub his feet. Then, he took a nap until 4:30 p.m. When he woke up, he had his supper, and would leave for a pool hall called LaFerla's on 13th and Briggs. It was a meeting place for all of the Old Italian immigrants. There, they would play cards and have some drinks. I didn't get to go with him, so I anxiously awaited his return home. He usually left LaFerla's around 8:30 p.m. My aunts and Nana had fresh doughnuts and rolls waiting for him. After enjoying the baked goods, he just got up, went to bed, and never said anything to anyone. Some nights he grunted at his wife. That meant she had to come to bed with him. The women today think they have it rough!

Questions

1. This reading is mainly about two people. Who are they?

   _____

2. What was the author's purpose for writing this memoir?

   _____

   _____

   _____

3. Make a short list of the sequence of events.

   _____

   _____

   _____

   _____

4. What transition words or phrases did you notice?

   _____

   _____

B. Cause and Effect

PREPARING TO READ Have you ever recognized how one action can create a result that is positive or negative? An author uses the Cause and Effect pattern to show relationships among events. A cause can create many effects, and an effect can be due to several causes. As you read the essay below, identify what the author says can cause a lack of literacy proficiency. Next, identify what happens as a result of the lack of literacy proficiency.

CAN LITERACY HELP A PERSON AVOID FRUSTRATION?

Illiteracy is a national problem. Illiteracy is the inability to communicate proficiently and effectively through reading and writing. There are several things, or combinations of things, which can lead to this problem. A big issue is the fact that parents with little schooling usually do not create activities for their children centered around reading and writing. Also, those parents don't usually spend their money on books for the home. Even though it is often misunderstood, the message the children receive is that reading and writing are not important issues for their family. Most parents have no clue that their children might be internalizing the message that reading and writing are unimportant. They simply do not want their children to see their lack of skills, and in turn, the children follow in their parents' footsteps. However, because the Emergent Literacy Theory relies on the stimulation of the interrelated activities between reading and writing, caregivers who do not demonstrate literacy skills needed for development later discover their children might not value reading and writing in the ways they hoped. Another problem some families face is a lack of financial resources. As young people grow, they see this lack of money and some feel a need to drop out of school in order to contribute to the family's stability. Neither the parents nor the young person realize the large gap this will create in the area of literacy. Learning disabilities are another factor that create complicated problems for literacy learning. The children and teens might get extra help at school, but might not get the help at home needed to overcome their disabilities. This is not because the parents do not want to help; instead, it's because those parents do not know how to help. Often, people with a lack of resources and some of the aforementioned problems tend to suffer from functional illiteracy. Functional illiteracy is hard to define, but at its core it means the person is not completely illiterate. He or she can order from a menu, read street signs, sign agreements, and perform low-level reading and writing tasks, but might not be able to read a book or newspaper.

The effects of being functionally illiterate can best be described as "living in frustration." It is virtually impossible to obtain all the information needed to function successfully in the complex written world around us. Often, functionally illiterate people find themselves unable to secure employment other than at low-income jobs. Usually, these jobs have no advancement opportunities and do nothing to help a person develop into a stronger employee. Also, these types of jobs often do not have benefits, such as paid sick time or medical insurance. The people who must accept these jobs find themselves in unfortunate situations, often with no options. It is common for functionally illiterate people to sign leases without understanding them. Also, they are easy targets for scammers because they get lost in the written material. This creates an embarrassing situation for them, so they do not ask for explanations or assistance from others. They just suffer the consequences. In turn, people who are functionally illiterate suffer low self-esteem and all the vulnerabilities that come with it.

Community colleges offer people a new start coupled with wraparound support services that help bridge literacy gaps. Low-income workers or people with literacy gaps often turn to community colleges in hopes of completing a certificate or degree program that can lead to better wages and an overall healthier workday. However, the literacy road is difficult and some students with literacy gaps give up too quickly. The ones who persevere will be the first to tell the frustrated student, "Stick it out; education is something no one can ever take away from you. Education builds confidence, which employers recognize and value."

Questions

1. What situations does the author suggest can lead to functional illiteracy (causes)?

   _____

   _____

2. What does the author suggest it is like for people to live with functional illiteracy (effects)?

   _____

   _____

3. Write a summary sentence showing a relationship between reading and writing as a child and valuing reading and writing as an adult.

   _____

   _____

   _____

4. What transition words did you notice?

   _____

   _____

C. Process Analysis

PREPARING TO READ   Have you ever thought about the steps involved in scientifically proving something? As you read, notice how the author lays out the steps in the process. Sometimes, the steps will be imbedded in the text, but the outcome for the reader is the same—to pull out the steps needed to complete the process.

THE SCIENTIFIC METHOD

The Scientific Method is a framework for studying and learning more about the world around you. It is a method used when trying to collect data and record observations in the hopes of forming a logical conclusion about a subject, topic, or idea. The steps in the Scientific Method provide a solid guideline to follow when conducting a scientific inquiry. The steps below outline and describe the Scientific Method.

Observation

An observation has been made when a person experiences an event that encourages him or her to answer why or how it happened that way.

Question

In the Scientific Method, a question converts general wonder and interest to a purpose-driven thinking activity that can be investigated through an experiment.

Hypothesis

A hypothesis is an informed guess as to the possible answer to the question presented. The purpose of the hypothesis is not to arrive at the perfect answer; the purpose is to provide a direction for the experiment. Having the hypothesis, or intended outcome, in mind will work as a guide to help set up the experiment.

Experiment

The experiment is one of the most important steps, as it is used to prove the hypothesis right or wrong. In order to be accepted as scientific proof, an experiment must meet certain conditions—it must be controlled and have the ability to be reproduced so that it can be tested for errors.

Data

As the experiment is conducted, collect data. Then, analyze all the data.

Conclusion

The data is used to decide if the hypothesis is proved or disproved. If the data proves the hypothesis correct, the question is answered. However, if the data disproves the hypothesis, the scientific inquiry begins again with this observation leading to a new hypothesis.

Questions

1. What does the word "inquiry" mean?

   _____

   _____

2. In order, list and provide a summary phrase of each step a person should take when making a scientific inquiry.

   _____

   _____

   _____

   _____

   _____

   _____

   _____

3. Why is order the steps are written in so important to the reader?

   _____

   _____

   _____

D. Classification

PREPARING TO READ   Think of any topic and how you would break it down into *categories* or groups. The following article is divided into time periods related to the brutal German Holocaust. As you read, notice that the format is similar to that of a textbook. Many textbooks are written in this manner. Please refer to Chapter 3 for information on reading textbooks.

THE HOLOCAUST IN GERMANY

In the Beginning

For centuries, the Jewish people had been thought by some as being inferior to other people. They were made fun of, ostracized, and belittled. This idea became "accepted" by some, leading to many people becoming desensitized to the treatment of Jews. As the poor treatment escalated and Adolf Hitler gained power, the Jewish population endured some of the most hateful human treatment in world history.

The first step in the annihilation of Jews began with the Germans. Led by dictator Adolf Hitler, the German soldiers rounded up the Jews and created "Jewish residential districts," which became known as "ghettos." These ghettos were characterized by hunger, disease, and overcrowding. The winters were bitterly cold, but the Jewish people did not have the necessary supplies to keep warm. The Germans collected all items that could possibly be fashioned into weapons, which made the Jews vulnerable and weak. Even in the midst of these horrible conditions, many ghetto residents fought against the German's goal of dehumanizing them. Parents continued to educate their children even though it was against the law and unjustly punishable. Some residents held clandestine religious services and observed Jewish holidays. The Jewish people did not know that the creation of these ghettos was the preliminary step to sending them to concentration camps and ultimately killing them.

The Escalation That Opened the Door to the End

Beginning in 1941, Jews from all over the continent were transported to the ghettos. The German invasion of the Soviet Union in June 1941 began a new level of brutality for the Jewish people. Despite the fact they were outgunned and outnumbered by the hundreds, young Jewish men and women began to fight back. They knew they would not be successful, but would have some honor in knowing they resisted the atrocities for all Jews. During the summer of 1944, when the end of the war for Germany was clear, large populations of Jews were taken to Auschwitz. As many as 12,000 Jews were killed every day at the concentration camp. By the spring of 1945, allies of Hitler began seeking to distance themselves and take power from him. Before he committed suicide, he urged the German leaders and people to follow "the strict observance of the racial laws and with merciless resistance against the universal poisoners of all peoples"–the Jews. Germany formally surrendered May 8, 1945, one week after Hitler took his own life.

A Homeland for Jewish Survivors

There were increasing pressures on the Allied Powers to find a homeland for the Jewish survivors. As Great Britain recognized the right of the Jewish people to establish a "national home," Palestine was split into two areas. The modern State of Israel was announced on the day the last British forces left Israel, May 14, 1948.

Questions

1. Why would the author break the essay into these three parts?

_____

_____

_____

2. How do the subheadings help the reader keep the information organized while reading?

_____

_____

_____

E. Comparison/Contrast

PREPARING TO READ   Compare (same) and contrast (different) readings show how two or more subjects are the same and how they differ. As you read, look for the similarities and differences between the traits of successful students and the traits of struggling students.

WHAT MAKES STUDENTS DIFFERENT?

Have you ever wondered why some students succeed and some students don't? As they come through the door of the college, they are all equipped with their backpacks, supplies, and skills. What changes when the due date of the assignments come? Could it be their backpacks? No. Could it be their supplies? Maybe. If a student chooses not to buy a course book, that could change things. Could it be skills? Yes. Some students have what I like to call "stick-with-it-ness." And sadly, some students have what I like to call "make-an-exception-for-me-ness." What is the difference between the two?

Students who possess "stick-with-it-ness" have a secret. They value education and understand its purpose for their adult life. They are committed to coming to class. When they come to class, they are prepared and organized. If they have a personal problem, they leave it outside the classroom door. They look up information they don't understand and ask appropriate questions when needed. They try to pull together their new knowledge with their old knowledge to make informed decisions. Lastly, they have an "I CAN" attitude.

Students who possess "make-an-exception-for-me-ness" lack the secret. They have ambitions just like the successful students, but what they lack is the knowledge of how a college education gets them to where they see themselves in their adult life. They do not understand the steps that will help them achieve their ambitions. Often, these students are late for class on a regular basis. They also struggle with poor attendance. They struggle with priorities and sometimes have so much going on outside of school that they can't keep up with the demands of the classroom. Their lack of preparation shows an instructor that they don't understand the value of being in a college classroom. They tend to want to memorize information instead of thinking about and analyzing a situation. They have an "I CAN'T" attitude.

In conclusion, successful students try to understand and grasp college culture whereas unsuccessful students struggle to figure out the system and what is going on around them. If the "I CAN'T" students could just change their mantra to "I CAN," it is my belief that we would see a marked improvement in college entrance course grades.

Questions

1. What traits do successful students possess, according to the author?

   _____

   _____

   _____

2. What traits do unsuccessful students possess, according to the author?

   _____

   _____

   _____

3. What are similarities between the two groups?

   _____

   _____

F. Definition and Example

PREPARING TO READ   Have you ever thought about the difference between thinking and critical thinking? As you read, create a definition for "Critical Thinking" from the author's words. Then, notice all the examples provided to further explain "Critical Thinking". Record the examples.

WHAT IS CRITICAL THINKING?

By Linda Elder (September 2007)

Critical thinking is self-guided, self-disciplined thinking which attempts to reason at the highest level of quality in a fair-minded way. People who think critically consistently attempt to live rationally, reasonably, empathically. They are keenly aware of the inherently flawed nature of human thinking when left unchecked. They strive to diminish the power of their egocentric and socio-centric tendencies. They use the intellectual tools that critical thinking offers – concepts and principles that enable them to analyze, assess, and improve thinking. They work diligently to develop the intellectual virtues of intellectual integrity, intellectual humility, intellectual civility, intellectual empathy, intellectual sense of justice and confidence in reason.

They realize that no matter how skilled they are as thinkers, they can always improve their reasoning abilities and they will always at times fall prey to mistakes in reasoning, human irrationality, prejudices, biases, distortions, uncritically accepted social rules and taboos, self-interest, and vested interest. They strive to improve the world in whatever ways they can and contribute to a more rational, civilized society. At the same time, they recognize the complexities often inherent in doing so.

They strive never to think simplistically about complicated issues and always consider the rights and needs of relevant others. They recognize the complexities in developing as thinkers, and commit themselves to life-long practice toward self-improvement. They embody the Socratic principle: The unexamined life is not worth living, because they realize that many unexamined lives together result in an uncritical, unjust, dangerous world.

Questions

1. According to the author, what is critical thinking?

_____

_____

_____

_____

_____

2. Create a list of examples the author used to further explain critical thinking.

_____

_____

_____

_____

_____

3. Explain how the examples help you better understand the definition.

_____

_____

_____

_____

_____

There are other commonly used patterns of organization. Three more are briefly described below and include cause and effect, spatial order, and simple list.

Description

Definition: The description pattern is used when the author is painting a picture for the reader with words. The words will appeal to the reader's five senses. If the author has done a good job, the reader will visualize whatever it is the author wants her to see.

Example: Western State Colorado University is located in the city of Gunnison, which is in one of the most aesthetically pleasing areas of Colorado. The road leading to the city is wound very tightly around a steep mountain. The college sits in a little valley at the top. Everywhere you look, you can see mountains. The air smells clean, fresh, and free of pollutants. Western College sits right next to bustling boutiques, coffee shops, and mountain gear stores. In this "business district" of Gunnison, you can hear shoppers, bike horns, country music, and lots of young people chatting over coffee. Tourists flock to this area for skiing, sight-seeing, and hiking.

Spatial Order

Definition: This pattern tells you where things are physically positioned and/or how the area is arranged.

Example: There are many things I love about our neighborhood, but the one thing that stands out most is the way the developer created that down home, yet affluent, feeling. As you drive into our neighborhood, there's a huge fountain with iron gates on each side of it. The entrance is paved with bricks. As you continue to drive down the main street you see beautiful landscaped yards on either side of the road. Halfway down, there's a gazebo, a fishing pond, and a huge green field with a walking track all the way around it. This is a congregational area for all of the neighbors. The kids fish while the parents walk around the track and visit with one another. As you exit our neighborhood on that same main road, you drive right into a gas station, with a sub sandwich shop on the left, a coffee shop on the right, and a great big carwash behind it all!

Simple List

Definition: This pattern uses words and sentences instead of numbers for items that are listed. The list actually becomes the details.

Example: There are several ways to get your dogs to stop barking. One way is to use a shock collar. Some people think it is cruel, but the next-door neighbors love the idea! Another way is to fill a can with pennies and shake it by the dog's ears when he is consistently barking. This actually works wonders rather quickly. Lastly, you can put hot sauce and water in a spray bottle and spray the dog when his barking becomes offensive. We do not recommend this one, though we have heard of several people using the method.

Writing Like a Reader

In this chapter, you learned how an author uses "patterns" to write. When a reader can recognize the author's pattern, comprehension is easier because the reader knows how to follow the author's message. Remember that often patterns are mixed throughout any piece of writing. When you're writing using different patterns, the glue that holds it all together is transition words, which are also called signal words. Without these words, the reader has a more difficult time comprehending. Transition words are often a single word, but sometimes they can be several words used in a phrase. Transition words are like signs along the reading road, so when you write, be sure to give your readers the signs they need to follow the road to comprehension!

For example, read the short paragraph below without any transition, or signal, words. Then read it with transition, or signal, words.

> *Registering for college classes is simple. Fill out your forms. Turn them in to the appropriate people. Print your schedule. Go get your books. Go to your classes. Pay the bill.*

OR

> *Registering for college classes is simple. First, fill out your forms. Second, turn them in to the appropriate people. Then, print a copy of your schedule and take it to the bookstore to get your books. Next, go to your classes. Finally, pay the bill.*

The second paragraph is much more unified than the first because of the use of transition words.

Chapter Summary

Patterns of Organization: A pattern refers to how the sentences or ideas in a reading are structured or arranged. Recognizing the different patterns leads to improved comprehension.

Transition Words: Provide a bridge from one idea to another.

Narration: A story or event usually told in first person. Tells who, what, why, when, and where. The sequence of events is important.

Cause and Effect: Shows the relationship between events. Helps the reader see connections.

Process Analysis: Shows with words a method of doing something. The sequence is extremely important. Look for steps and order.

Classification: Divides a subject into various categories. Identifies a member or group based on similar characteristics. Look for part-to-whole relationships or various categories into which a large number of items can be sorted.

Comparison/Contrast: Shows how two things are alike and/or different. The two things may be compared and contrasted subject by subject, or be compared and contrasted point by point.

Definition: Defines a person, place, thing, or idea by explaining the characteristics that distinguish it from others in its class.

Check Your Learning (Learning Outcomes)

Have you mastered the Learning Objectives (LOs) for Chapter 6? Place a check mark next to each LO that you're able to do.

_____ LO1—Recognize different patterns of organization

_____ LO2—Identify the organization within each pattern

_____ LO3—Analyze information from each pattern

_____ LO4—Understand the purpose of each pattern

Go back and review the sections that cover any LO you didn't check.

Quick Connections—Chapter Six

NEWS SOURCE CONNECTION

Narration: Using a newspaper or news magazine, locate a narrative selection. Make sure to remember that in news reporting the patterns are often intermixed, and a narrative is a retelling of an event. Clip the article from the newspaper or news magazine (print, if an online article) and highlight the example.

Cause and Effect: Using a newspaper or news magazine, locate an article or part of an article that shows the relationship between two events; one which led to the other. The newspaper is filled with this pattern. With cause and effect, the reader is looking for relationships among events. Often, the headline will read as an effect or a cause, and the body of the article will state the causes or the effects. Clip the article from the newspaper or news magazine (if you are looking at an online article, print it) and highlight the example.

Process: Using a newspaper or news magazine, locate an article describing a process. As you read, you're looking for gradual steps or changes that lead to a final result. Clip the article from the newspaper or news magazine (print, if an online article) and highlight the example.

Classification: Using a newspaper or news magazine, locate an article which includes an example of classification. You're reading to find information that has been divided into categories. Clip the article from the newspaper or news magazine (print, if an online article) and highlight the example.

Comparison/Contrast: Using newspapers or newsmagazines, locate two stories related to the same topic. Create a chart or diagram to compare and contrast their similarities and differences.

Definition: Using a newspaper or news magazine, locate an article that defines a person, place, thing, or idea. You're reading to find information that identifies someone or something by distinct, clear, and detailed essential qualities. Clip the article from the newspaper or news magazine (print, if an online article) and highlight the example.

TEXTBOOK CONNECTION

Narration: Using one of your own textbooks, locate a narrative selection. A narrative is retelling of an event. Mark the section within the text. Show your teacher to confirm.

Cause and Effect: Using one of your own textbooks, locate a passage showing a cause and effect relationship. Mark the section within the text with sticky notes. Show your teacher or share with a group to confirm.

Process: Using one of your own textbooks, locate a passage describing a process. As you read, you're looking for gradual steps or changes that lead to a final result. Mark the section within the text. Show your teacher or share with a group to confirm.

Classification: Using one of your own textbooks, locate a passage which includes an example of classification. You're reading to find information that has been divided into categories. Mark the section within the text. Show your teacher or share with a group to confirm.

Comparison/Contrast: Using two of your own textbooks, compare and contrast them based on various factors such as: Where are the chapter words defined? What types of visuals are included (pictures, graphs, charts, etc.)? Are there chapter summaries?

Definition: Using one of your own textbooks, locate a passage that defines a person, place, thing, or idea. You're reading to find information that identifies someone or something by distinct, clear, and detailed essential qualities. Mark the section within the text. Show your teacher or share with a group to confirm.

NOVEL CONNECTION

Narration: Choose a particular event, told in narrative style, that happened within a novel. Retell the event to the class, or you may choose to write it.

Cause and Effect: Using a novel, choose a character that has experienced a cause and effect situation. Paraphrase the situation verbally or in a written document.

Process: Using a problem from a novel, identify steps a character could use to solve the problem.

Classification: Using a novel, create a category chart for the characters, events, problems, emotions, heroes, villains, and so on.

Comparison/Contrast: Using two characters from a course novel, compare and contrast them.

Definition: Choose an idea or topic from a novel. Create a list of characteristics the author uses to define it.

WEB CONNECTION

Using an online magazine or newspaper, read to locate examples of each of the six patterns described in this chapter.

Seven

Visual Literacy Strategies

Chapter Preview

Visual Literacy Strategies Overview
A. Cluster Diagram
B. Five Ws Concept Web
C. Venn Diagram
D. KWL Chart

LEARNING OBJECTIVES (LOs)

Upon completion of this chapter, you'll be able to:

■ LO1—Organize pertinent information in a reading

■ LO2—Extract main ideas from a reading

■ LO3—Use graphic organizer strategies to enhance comprehension

*A graphic organizer is worth
a thousand words . . .*

Readiness Quiz

1. Read the article below. After reading, fill out the visual organizer.
2. As a class or group, discuss extraction of the pertinent information from the article using the 5Ws chart.

ANIMAL HOMELESSNESS

Animal homelessness is a problem that causes animals' lives to be lost to euthanasia, poses a public safety concern, and costs taxpayers money to pay for services to deal with stray, abandoned, and feral animals and their offspring. It has been proven that the sterilization of animals decreases not only the number of homeless and feral animals born each year, but it also decreases unwanted behavior in animals, including roaming and aggression, which can lead to the surrender and euthanasia of animals. One solution to this problem is offsetting the cost of spaying/neutering animals. Another is standardizing and requiring animal control officer training to create uniform and stronger enforcement of animal control laws. The Department of Agricultural Resources has recently been granted an opportunity to address this important issue, and now the public can help.

On October 31, 2012, a new law took effect that, in part, created the Massachusetts Homeless Animal Prevention and Care Fund (Massachusetts Animal Fund). The Fund is administered by the Massachusetts Department of Agricultural Resources and assisted by an advisory committee and seeks to end the problem of animal homelessness in Massachusetts.

5Ws Chart

Who was involved? _____

_____

What actually happened? _____

Why did it happen? _____

_____

When did it happen? _____

_____

Where did it happen? _____

How did it happen? _____

VISUAL LITERACY STRATEGIES OVERVIEW

There are many kinds of visual images that can be used to represent information, and there are various ways information can be organized, depending upon the material being read. One of the most common types of visual literacy tool is some form of graphic organizer. A graphic organizer works well to simplify and organize material visually in one or more of the following ways:

- According to topics, main ideas, and details
- In sequential order
- To show relationships between or among different things
- To show similarities and differences between two or more ideas or things
- By story elements
- . . . and many others!

Graphic organizers come in numerous forms. We will present three of the most widely used examples in this text, but there are many more examples on the Internet if you search for *graphic organizers.*

How Do They Work?

Graphic organizers provide visual representations of ideas, facts, theories, and concepts. They consist of circles, boxes, and other shapes, along with lines, to show connections. Creating a graphic organizer not only assists you in preparing and studying for a test, but it can also provide you with a memorable visual *during* the test. Two features of an effective graphic organizer are **elaboration** and **personalization.** *Elaboration* is the use of colors, designs, and pictures to aid in memory. *Personalization* involves creating associations to the information on your graphic organizer with personal pictures or designs that make sense to you. These images will help you remember what is important. Following are descriptions of three common graphic organizers.

1. THE CLUSTER DIAGRAM   A cluster diagram has many uses, but is best used for organizing main ideas and details from textbook chapters. To complete a cluster diagram for a textbook chapter, the student would begin with the title of the chapter near the center of the page. Each additional line from the center with a circle at the end would represent a main idea from that chapter. Lines added from each main idea circle would represent major details the student should remember from the chapter. Use of colors and small pictures or graphics may also enhance memory. A cluster diagram allows students to see the "chunks" of information they need to know.

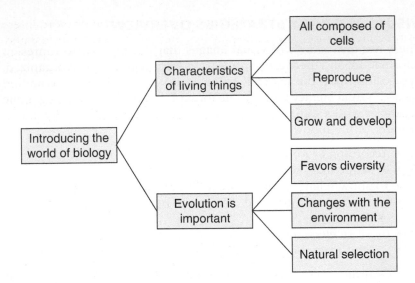

2. THE 5 WS CONCEPT WEB The concept web is a gathering place for information. It is most effective when used with a narrative or news article. The "five Ws" concept web is a graphic organizer that consists of circles or squares and branches to other circles or squares. Each circle represents a specific "W." The center circle represents the title. The additional lines with circles and/or squares represent specific "Ws." The great thing about graphic organizers is that you can add lines and shapes to suit the material you're reading.

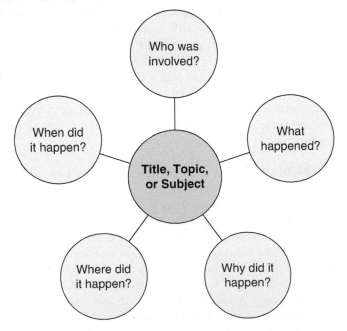

3. THE VENN DIAGRAM A Venn Diagram is a set of two or more intersecting circles. It is a way to display information in a visual format and to categorize information into groups: most commonly, similarities and differences. You can use this diagram as you read to separate two or more ideas. The center is where you would write what the ideas have in common. Another way to use this tool is as a thought organizer before you write a compare and contrast paragraph or essay.

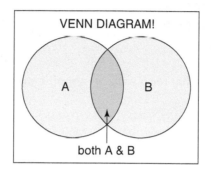

To Practice

Use the following readings and graphic organizers for practice.

- Cluster Diagram: Obsessive-Compulsive Disorder
- 5 Ws Concept Web: Social Media-Your Online Reputation
- Venn Diagram: High School and College

QUICK TIP

Remember information by using **elaboration** (designs, colors, patterns) and **personalization** (association to something familiar, pictures).

QUICK TIP

When material seems disorganized or poorly organized, pay more attention to the headings, and read the summary first (if one is provided).

QUICK TIP

Font size is generally an important clue to organizing information. A main heading in large font often indicates a main point. Each sub-heading in smaller font is an important point supporting the main point. When the font reverts to large again, you have a new idea, or the next main point.

FOR EXTRA PRACTICE

Use the readings in Chapter 6 with the graphic organizers provided in this chapter.

A. Cluster Diagram

Use the cluster diagram that follows the article "Obsessive-Compulsive Disorder."

1. Before reading, place the title of the reading in the center circle.
2. After and during reading, place the main ideas of the reading in the circles directly linked to the title.
3. After and during reading, place the major details in the circles directly linked to each main idea.
4. Remember that you can add as many lines and circles/squares as you need when you create a cluster diagram.

OBSESSIVE-COMPULSIVE DISORDER

Mary Lynn Hendrix

What Is OCD?

In the mental illness called OCD, a person becomes trapped in a pattern of repetitive thoughts and behaviors that are senseless and distressing but extremely difficult to overcome. The following are typical examples of OCD:

> Troubled by the repeated thoughts that she may have contaminated herself by touching doorknobs and other "dirty" objects, a teenage girl spends hours every day washing her hands. Her hands are red and raw, and she has little time for social activities.
>
> A middle-aged man is tormented by the notion that he may injure others through carelessness. He has difficulty leaving his home because he must first go through a lengthy ritual of checking and rechecking the gas jets and water faucets to make certain that they are turned off.

If OCD becomes severe enough, it can destroy a person's capacity to function in the home, at work, or at school. That is why it is important to learn about the disorder and the treatments that are now available.

How Common Is OCD?

For many years, mental health professionals thought of OCD as a very rare disease because only a small minority of their patients had the condition. But it's believed that many of those afflicted with OCD, in efforts to keep their repetitive thoughts and behaviors secret, fail to seek treatment. This has lead to underestimates of the number of people with the illness. However, a recent survey by the National Institute of Mental Health (NIMH)—the Federal agency that supports research nationwide on the brain, mental illness, and mental health—has provided new understanding about the prevalence of OCD. The NIMH survey shows that this disorder may affect as much as 2 percent of the population, meaning that OCD is more common than schizophrenia and other severe mental illnesses.

Source: Building Strategies for College Reading, Prentice Hall, 2001.

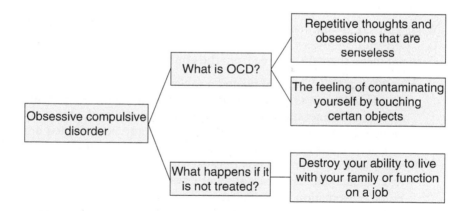

B. Five Ws Concept Web

1. Read "Social Media—Your Online Reputation" provided to students at Northeastern University.
2. After reading or as you read, use the concept web that follows the passage to fill in the who, what, why, when, and where of the reading.

SOCIAL MEDIA – YOUR ONLINE REPUTATION

Office of Information Security, Northeastern University

Social media is a great asset that can help to advance your career and goals. However, it also can hold you back. Close to 90 percent of hiring managers are looking at applicants' social media history and making hiring decisions based on what they find. The images and words you post can reach a much larger community than just your friends. Material sent to a small group of close friends might find its way onto the Internet where it becomes public forever. What some might find acceptable could offend others, and there can be very public consequences.

Below are some examples of how posts on social media have backfired, costing people their jobs and reputations. You will also find suggestions for how to scrub your social media profile and avoid potential problems.

Who is looking at your profile?

- College recruiters
- Rental agencies and landlords
- Job and co-op recruiters, and hiring managers
- Work supervisors and colleagues
- Loan and financial managers
- Social contacts – friends, family, and people you are dating

What you write and post matters . . .

What you say online has consequences. The First Amendment to the U.S. Constitution gives you the right to say most anything. However, it does not mean that you are free from the consequences of your speech.

- In 2011, a UCLA student posted a racist rant in a YouTube video. The backlash was swift and immediate, and she was publicly ridiculed online and on television. She quickly took down the video and apologized, but the post had already been copied and reposted elsewhere. The University did not discipline her but she withdrew from campus because of the controversy.
- In 2010, a Duke University student created a very detailed Power-Point presentation including names, pictures, and details of the men she had sex with at school. This document was only supposed to go to three friends but within a few days it was leaked to the Internet. The student not only embarrassed herself but also violated the privacy of the 13 people on the list. Forever, now future employers and others can view this information. There is no word on whether or not the student was sued by the 13 men because all parties have kept a low profile on the Internet since the incident.
- In 2009, a UCLA grad student was hired at Cisco and tweeted, "Cisco just offered me a job! Now I have to weigh the utility of a fatty paycheck against the daily commute to San Jose and hating the work." Unfortunately, the tweet was read by a hiring manager at Cisco and because the student was going to "hate the work," the company rescinded the employment offer.

- In 2011, a NYU Law and Security fellow tweeted what he thought was a funny joke about the brutal sexual assault of a reporter in Egypt. The backlash was swift, and in less than 24 hours he resigned from the university.
- In December 2011, three Capitol Hill legislative assistants were fired for tweets they sent detailing unprofessional behavior, drinking, and bad mouthing their boss.

Pictures

It might be fun to post pictures from your phone during a party on Facebook or Twitter, but who else besides your friends is viewing the pictures?

In 2008, a New England Patriots cheerleader was fired after she was seen in Facebook photos holding a sharpie next to a passed out man who was covered with drawn-on graffiti including swastikas and crude sexual drawings.

In 2011, two New York politicians—Anthony Weiner and Christopher Lee—were both forced to resign after they posted semi-nude pictures of themselves to Twitter and Craigslist.

Job and Co-op Implications

A 2011 survey by Rappler, a social media monitoring service, found that 91 percent of employers view an applicant's' social media profile and 69 percent have rejected an applicant because of what was posted on their social media sites.

The most common reasons for rejecting an applicant were:

- Posted inappropriate photos and comments
- Posted content about drinking and drugs
- Posted negative comments about a previous employer
- Demonstrated poor communication skills
- Lied about his or her qualifications

Your Date WILL Google You

A recent study reported that 43 percent of singles have Googled their dates before going out. First impressions are important and now they occur before the date begins. What does your profile say about you? Does your online persona differ from your personality? Are there images or posts that would be embarrassing to bring up with a new person you are trying to impress?

Recommendations to Clean Up Your Profile

- Remove any offending or questionable images and posts from your profile. Use your gut; if you think it might be questionable, remove it.
- Un-tag all images you are linked in and ask your friends to un-tag you in their pictures. If they refuse, "un-friend" them. Real friends care about your requests. You might also be able to change the settings on your account to make it harder for others to tag you in pictures or comments without your permission.
- Remove any questionable third party comments or links from your profile.
- Ask people at parties not to take your picture and not to upload pictures of you to the Internet.
- Do not post or respond in anger; stop, take a few breaths, and think about what you are going to write.
- When posting a picture of, or information about, another person, ask for permission first.
- Don't say bad things about your current or past employers and businesses.
- Keep your posts generally positive; leave out the profanity.
- Don't friend your boss, professor, or colleagues. Those people might be friendly in a work or school environment, but that does not mean it's appropriate to bring them into your private life.
- Keep constant tabs on all your social media accounts for new pictures or comments by others that do not show you in a positive light.
- Monitor the privacy settings on your social media accounts so that only your friends can see your posts (instead of friends-of-friends, and so on). Note that even with these privacy settings in place, anyone who has seen your information could potentially copy and re-post data without your permission. Choose your "friends" carefully.
- Do not accept friend requests from people you don't know even if they appear to be a friend of a friend. They could be spammers, marketing companies, data gathering companies, or others trying to collect personal information about you.
- **Nothing on the Internet is private; everything on the Internet is permanent.**

For more information or to read other articles like this, visit the webpage below.

http://www.northeastern.edu/securenu/social-media-your-online-reputation/

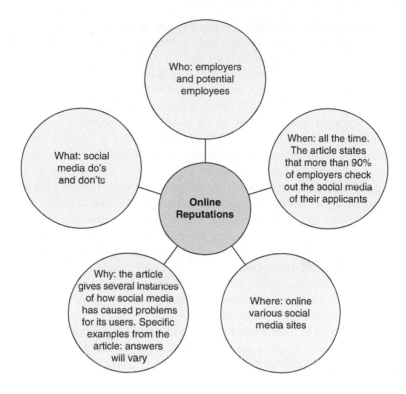

C. Venn Diagram

1. Read the essay "High School and College."
2. After reading or as you read, use the Venn Diagram graphic organizer that follows the story to list similarities and differences.

HIGH SCHOOL AND COLLEGE

When students graduate from high school, they are ready to make their college debut. As arrangements are made to enter the chosen college, students often wonder if college will be like high school. Some students are excited about this impending new adventure, while others are nervous and apprehensive. No matter which category applies, one thing is sure. While there are many similarities between high school and college, there are incredible differences.

In high school, a bell rings, and students fill the hallways on their way to first-period class. In college, a class begins at a certain time; you are either there or you're not. While one instructor may allow you to enter class late, another instructor may decide not to let you in at all. If you have a pattern of tardies in high school, you usually receive an after-school detention. If you're habitually tardy in college, however, your instructor may drop you from the course or lower your grade. If you're absent in high school, your parents may need to call and inform the school. And if you're *excessively* absent, your parents may receive a letter in the mail from the school district. In college, although you generally can be absent a certain number of times, once that predetermined number has been reached, the instructor may drop you from the course.

In high school, there's often a person in charge of student discipline. Students may be sent to an in-school suspension room for not completing assignments, for disrupting class, or for fighting with other students. In college, students simply are expected not to create any of these problems. Additionally, while high school teachers may be responsible for writing referrals, sending students out of the room, and explaining an issue to a student's parents, college instructors merely may ask a student either to get the work done or to drop the class. If a student does not comply, the *instructor* is able to drop the student from class. Also, if college students disrupt a class or fight, they may be asked to leave the classroom. If students resist, a college instructor has the option of calling campus security to receive help in removing them.

In conclusion, good attendance habits, timely completion of work, and responsible classroom behavior are factors that enable students to be successful *both* in high school and in college. High school students, however, receive much more direct support from teachers, counselors, and administrators to ensure that they graduate and receive their high school diplomas. College students, on the other hand, must learn to take full advantage of available guidance, opportunities, and assistance in order to graduate and earn a college degree. While much support is still attainable, the ultimate responsibility for college success lies with the student.

Now that you've read "High School and College," fill in the Venn Diagram that follows.

Bells ring to move students, receive after-school detention for tardies, parents must call when you are absent, excessive absences addressed by a letter in the mail, there is a person in charge of discipline, a student can receive in-school suspension, receive more direct support from teachers, counselors, and administrators

Good attendance habits, timely completion of work, and responsible classroom behavior are success factors.

Students must arrive at their classes on time on their own, some instructors won't let tardy students into their classes, you can be dropped from classes for being excessively late or absent, college students are not expected to cause discipline problems, an instructor can remove a student or withdraw a student for not being appropriate in class, instructors can use campus security for uncooperative students, a student's college success is the ultimate responsibility of the student

D. KWL Chart

The KWL chart begins with you recording your background knowledge about the topic of the reading (what I know). The next column is dedicated to what you hope to learn (what I want to know). As you read, answer the questions and record new things you didn't know before (what I learned). This strategy helps you read the piece closely and connect it to what you already know. This chart can be used for just about any type of reading. It is a great tool to use in all academic courses. It looks simple, but it is a very powerful resource.

Topic _____		
What I Know	**What I Want to Know**	**What I Learned**

Writing Like a Reader

In Chapter 2, you learned how to identify main ideas and details. What you actually did was sharpen your skills in "deconstructing" a paragraph. That is what a reader does. As a writer, you're "constructing" paragraphs. A well-written paragraph should have three things. The first is a main idea, which is the point the writer wants to get across to the reader. Second, it must have some major details. The major details support the main idea or the point the writer is making. Think of major details as "evidence." Most paragraphs also have a third component called minor details. A minor detail tells the reader more about the major detail it follows. The writer uses minor details to help the reader understand the "evidence" better. Use the **Paragraph Plan** graphic organizer below to create your own paragraph. Focus on learning the difference between destructing (reading) and constructing (writing).

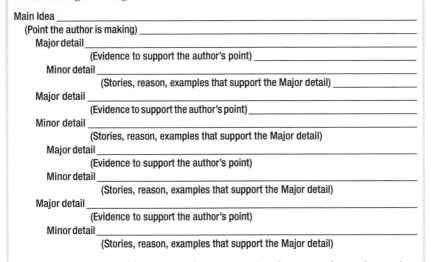

Main Idea _____
  (Point the author is making) _____
    Major detail _____
        (Evidence to support the author's point) _____
     Minor detail _____
        (Stories, reason, examples that support the Major detail) _____
    Major detail _____
        (Evidence to support the author's point) _____
    Minor detail _____
        (Stories, reason, examples that support the Major detail)
     Major detail _____
        (Evidence to support the author's point)
    Minor detail _____
        (Stories, reason, examples that support the Major detail)
    Major detail _____
        (Evidence to support the author's point)
    Minor detail _____
        (Stories, reason, examples that support the Major detail)

Once you're able to see the connection between how the author constructs a paragraph and how the reader deconstructs it, your reading comprehension will increase dramatically, and so will your writing skills!

Chapter Summary

    Graphic Organizers: Graphic organizers are used to create visual representations of ideas, facts, theories, and concepts.

    Elaboration: Elaboration is the use of colors, designs, and pictures to aid in remembering information.

    Personalization: Personalization is creating associations to the information on your graphic organizer with personal pictures or designs that makes sense to you.

Cluster Diagram: A cluster diagram has many uses, but is best used for organizing main ideas and details from textbook chapters.

5 Ws Concept Web: A graphic organizer that helps to identify who the reading is about, what happened, why it happened, when it happened, and where it happened.

Venn Diagram: A graphic organizer that helps organize information according to similarities and differences.

KWL: When presented with any new reading, the KWL graphic organizer helps the reader access their background knowledge, set a purpose for reading, and record answers to their questions or new information they learned.

Check Your Learning (Learning Outcomes)

Have you mastered the Learning Objectives (LOs) for Chapter 7? Place a check mark next to each LO that you're able to do.

_____ LO1—Organize pertinent information in a reading

_____ LO2—Extract main ideas from a reading

_____ LO3—Use graphic organizer strategies to enhance comprehension

Go back and review the sections that cover any LO you didn't check.

Quick Connections—Chapter Seven

NEWS SOURCE CONNECTION

Using the concept web format located within the chapter, choose a newspaper or news magazine article. Read the article and complete a 5 Ws concept web.

TEXTBOOK CONNECTION

Choose one of your own textbooks. Use the cluster diagram located within this chapter. As you read the chapter, place the main ideas in the circles directly connected to the title. Place the major details in the circles directly connected to the main idea circles.

NOVEL CONNECTION

Using a novel, select two characters and create a Venn Diagram that lists their similarities and differences.

WEB CONNECTION

Go to a news source website such as *Time* magazine or the *New York Times* website. Find an article and create your own graphic organizer. Personalize it! Add color! Feel free to place information in ways that give meaning to you.

Eight

Information Literacy Strategies

Chapter Preview

Information Literacy Strategies Overview
A. How to Search the Internet
    1. The World Wide Web
    2. Four Key Components

LEARNING OBJECTIVES (LOs)

Upon completion of this chapter section, you'll be able to:

- LO1—Conduct an Internet search using the World Wide Web
- LO2—Differentiate between the four key components of an Internet search

Ability to use a computer to read and write in college . . . Priceless

B. Evaluating and Citing Web Sources
1. Does the Site Meet the Purpose of Your Search?
2. Is the Site Easy to Use? (Design and Navigability)
3. How Valid Is the Information Found?
4. When and How to Cite Web Sources

LEARNING OBJECTIVES (LOs)

Upon completion of this chapter section, you'll be able to:

■ LO1—Determine if a site meets the purpose of your search

■ LO2—Evaluate a site's design and navigability (ease of use)

■ LO3—Assess the validity of website information

■ LO4—Correctly cite Web sources

C. Word Processing Basics—A Reference Guide

LEARNING OBJECTIVES (LOs)

Upon completion of this chapter section, you'll be able to:

■ LO1—Review, as needed, some of the basic concepts of word processing using the reference guide in this section.

Strategy Area A: How to Search the Internet

Readiness Quiz A

Choose **T** for true and **F** for false after reading each statement below.

1. _____ A browser is a page that contains information, pictures, and video clips about a specific topic.

2. _____ A search engine is a computerized index to find information on the WWW.

3. _____ WWW is a math symbol, not a computer term.

4. _____ Opening a link from a Web page takes concentration and memory.

Note: If you're a beginner in the area of computer basics (especially word processing), you may want to check out the readiness quiz and accompanying reference guide in Strategy Area C of this chapter before starting Strategy Areas A and B of the chapter.

INFORMATION LITERACY STRATEGIES OVERVIEW

Today, we acquire information in a broadening variety of ways. To adapt to our ever-growing digital environment, we also need to broaden our reading strategies. Strategy Area A of this chapter will help you learn how to search for information, and Strategy Area B will help you determine which sites and sources contain reliable information. Once you know how to do both, you'll be able to use technology to find valid information on just about any topic. Strategy Area C covers some word processing basics and is a reference guide for those who might need that kind of assistance.

A. How to Search the Internet

The first strategy involved in reading on the Internet is searching for the information you want to read. You may need information for class assignments such as a research paper, a speech, or a presentation. In addition to class assignments, you also use the Internet for personal purposes such as researching colleges, career paths, or job opportunities. To find relevant information quickly, you need to know how to effectively search the Internet. The first section of this chapter will show you how to conduct an efficient Internet search.

1. THE WORLD WIDE WEB   The World Wide Web (commonly abbreviated as "the Web," "WWW," or "W3") is an interconnected, hypertext-based network that allows you to browse a variety of Internet resources organized by home pages. The Web is incredibly vast. This is positive because there's so much information available, but it can be negative because anyone with a little computer knowledge can create a Web page. When you do a search, you must realize that there's an extensive amount of unreliable, as well as reliable, information.

2. FOUR KEY COMPONENTS   There are four basic components you'll use to locate information on the Web.

> *Browser:* A browser is a computer program that provides a way of viewing the information on the Web. Major browsers include Microsoft's Internet Explorer, Apple's Safari, Google Chrome, and Mozilla Firefox.

> *Search Engine:* A computerized index to information on the Web.

> **Popular Search Engines**
>
> www.google.com
>
> www.bing.com
>
> www.yahoo.com

> *Web Page:* A document location or site that provides information on your search topic(s). It may contain pictures, video clips, audio clips, charts, graphs, links, and more.

QUICK TIP

Remember, anyone can make a Web page. When you search, use the strategies in Strategy Area B to make sure you find valid information.

Hyperlink (also called a hotlink): An automatic "address jump" to another site containing similar or more information on your search topic. Often a hyperlink will be in blue and underlined. However, the real defining feature is that the appearance of the text in a hyperlink changes when the cursor hovers over it. Just click on the hyperlink, and you're at a new website!

3. HOW TO BEGIN

1. Formulate a question based on your class assignment or personal research.
2. Choose the important words from the question or topic sentence.

    Question: What was the Revolutionary War and who was involved?
    Important words: Revolutionary War
3. Type the important words into the search box located on your search engine home page.

QUICK TIP

You may open and close several Web pages from your results until you find the one with the reliable information you're seeking.

Now you should be ready to try a search! Search the Internet to find answers to the questions that follow. Fill in the important words that you'll need to type into the search box, do the search, and then fill in the answer to each question.

1. **Question:** What is the difference between an isosceles triangle and a right triangle?

   Important words: _____

   Search It!

   Answer from results: _____

   _____

2. **Question:** Who wrote the classic novel *To Kill a Mockingbird?*

   Important words: _____

   Search it!

   Answer from results: _____

3. **Question:** Define, describe, and draw the three major rock types in earth science.

   Important words: _____

   Search it!

   Answer from results:

Rock Type	Definition	Drawing
1.		
2.		
3.		

4. **Question:** Compare and contrast Vegetarian and Vegan diets.

   Important words: _____

   Search it!

   Answer from results:

Vegetarian and Vegan Diets

Similarities	Differences

Strategy Area B: Evaluating and Citing Web Sources

Readiness Quiz B

Choose **T** for true or **F** for false after reading each statement below.

1. _____ Information found on the Internet is always current.

2. _____ It is primarily the instructor's responsibility to check the reliability and validity of information used in students' course assignments.

3. _____ The government regulates all Internet websites, so we know they're factual.

4. _____ Anyone can create a website and have it on the Internet.

5. _____ You can tell certain things about a website from its address.

6. _____ It's difficult to tell whether a website is someone's personal page.

Consider the following three questions when evaluating Internet websites:

1. Does the site meet the purpose of your search?
2. Is the site easy to use?
3. How valid is the information found?

1. DOES THE SITE MEET THE PURPOSE OF YOUR SEARCH? Don't just start your search by going to Google or Yahoo! and typing in a couple of words! You need to start by asking yourself, "What is the purpose of this search?" or "What is my research goal?" Once you've determined a research goal, you can screen sites by comparing them with your research goal. To determine your research goal, ask yourself questions like these: Do I want facts, opinions, reasoned arguments, statistics, narratives, eyewitness reports, or descriptions? Is the purpose of my search to find new ideas, or is it to find either factual or reasoned support for a position? Do I want to survey opinion? Do I want graphics, photos, or illustrations? Determine exactly what kind of information you need for your assignment. If you're not sure, check with your instructor before you determine your research goal.

QUICK TIP

Always set a research goal before you start your information search!

Here are some reliable academic databases that are accessible through most college libraries. Unlike a general search engine such as Google, databases provide information management in terms of accuracy and reliability.

- GENERAL ACADEMIC RESEARCH
  - EBSCOhost (Academic Search Premier)
  - eLibrary
  - LexisNexis Academic
- POPULAR AND CONTROVERSIAL ISSUES
  - SIRS Researcher
- VOCATIONAL/TECHNICAL
  - EBSCOhost (Vocational and Career Collection)
- EDUCATION
  - EBSCOhost (ERIC)
- BUSINESS
  - EBSCOhost (Business Source Elite)

Databases aren't the only acceptable sources for academic research. Online journals, magazines, podcasts, documentaries, and videos are other acceptable information resources. Just make sure you cite these sources according to your teacher's instructions. And don't forget—there are still the good, old print materials!

QUICK TIP

Many people use Wikipedia as a quick, easily accessible source for information. However, it is not considered a scholarly, credible or authoritative source. Why not? One reason is that anyone can edit the page. Also, there's no guarantee that the writer is an expert on the topic or that the content has undergone rigorous editorial review. It's perfectly acceptable to read a Wikipedia entry to get a quick overview of your research topic, as long as you follow it up by reading more scholarly sources. Often, such sources are among the references that Wikipedia articles cite, so make sure to read the "Notes" and/or "References" sections!

Once you've set your research goal, you can begin your search using the strategies in Strategy Area A of this chapter. As you open up sites that you're considering for your research, skim over each one to see if it seems to meet your research goal. If it appears to have the information you're looking for according to your goal, then you're ready to apply the next two strategies to see if the site is one you want to use.

2. IS THE SITE EASY TO USE? (DESIGN AND NAVIGABILITY)   There are several factors which should indicate rapidly how easy a site will be for you to use. The two major ones are the site's *design*, or set-up and appearance, and its *navigability*, or how easy it is to get around in the site. If the site appears confusing to you, you may want to look at alternative sites that are more user friendly.

A site's design includes factors such as colors, background, size and font of print, and graphics. Are these things pleasing to the eye and easy to see? Or are they jumbled and distracting? Is there a clear order for finding information, or does it seem confusing?

Navigability of a site is how easy it is for the user to get around in, or use, the site. The design of the site contributes to its navigability. Are the different sections of the site clearly marked and easy to find? Is there always a link back to the home page? Are links to other sites easily identified? Are the links "hot," meaning you can click on them and be taken to the linked site? Are the links up to date?

QUICK TIP

Quickly skim over the home page of a site to get a feel for it. Is it pleasing to your eye? Does it make sense to you? Does it seem easy to start finding information?

If your impressions of the site are favorable so far, continue on to the third strategy for evaluating the site: Is the information found on the site valid and acceptable for use with your assignment?

3. HOW VALID IS THE INFORMATION FOUND?   Determining the validity of the information on a website is the most important part of the evaluation process. If the information isn't reliable and valid, it doesn't matter if it fits your research goal or is easy to use; the site is worthless to you! Often the most important part of a process tends to be the most time consuming, but it doesn't have to be. Below are some quick ways to check the validity of a site. Start by finding the answers to these questions:

1. *Sponsor:* What kind of organization sponsors the site? The answer can be found by looking at the domain: the last three letters in the address, or URL (Uniform Resource Locator). Addresses which end with the letters .edu (education), .gov (government), .mil (military), or .org (nonprofit organization) are usually reputable sites. Addresses ending in .com or .net are commercial addresses, which mean they're generally trying to make money in some way. Information on these sites can be reliable, but you need to do more checking than you would on the nonprofit sites. Sites that are personal Web pages set up by individuals are the least likely to be reliable. A site that ends with ~*name* (a personal name), % *name*, or a name followed by the words *people, users*, or *members*, indicates a personal website—which means, be careful!! These sites, while not necessarily unreliable, require more investigation from the reader because the information isn't backed by a domain owner or publisher.

QUICK TIP

The last three letters of the URL, also known as the "domain," are the quickest way to judge validity of a website.

2. *Author:* Who's responsible for the information? The top or bottom of the Web page should identify the person responsible for putting it up and maintaining it (the Webmaster of the site). Look for the author's institutional affiliation or other credentials. Is there documentation of the author or a bibliography of his work?

   What are the author's credentials and reputation? If the author is an expert and is qualified to write about the information contained at the site, it should be clearly stated. Look for a link to background information about the author, or better yet, a résumé. Make sure information is truly produced by this expert, and isn't posted erroneously or fraudulently.

3. *Date:* How old is the information? Remember, wide use of the Internet has been around for more than ten years, so you can't automatically assume that information you find on the Net is current. Look for the date that the site was last revised, which is

usually found at the bottom of the home page. Even if the date is fairly recent, remember that it doesn't mean that all of the information on the site was revised on that date. However, a recent update may mean that the site is well maintained, which is a good indicator of current information.

4. *Content:* Where did the information originate? What seems to be the purpose of the site? Again, the last three letters of the address tell you a lot about the source of the information and if the site is commercial or nonprofit. This is a good place to use your skimming skills. A quick skim of a few pages should help you begin to determine the comprehensiveness of the material, its accuracy, whether it contains more fact or opinion, if it's written from a scholarly point of view, if it seems to be promoting a particular viewpoint, or if it's advertising. Check to see if the information is documented in some way. Is there a bibliography or other list of sources? Has anyone reviewed the site? Keep in mind that there are specialized guide sites on the Internet to help you. These change frequently, so use your Internet searching skills to find the latest guides to Internet resources.

QUICK TIP

ALWAYS check the validity of a site before using it for academic purposes. Don't risk getting a low grade for using incorrect information.

5. *Corroboration:* Did you corroborate your sources? Corroboration, or finding the information in more than one place, is an important test of truth. It's a good idea to triangulate your sources—that is, find at least three sources that agree. If the sources do not agree, do further research to find out how wide the disagreement is before you draw your conclusions. If you can't find other sites with the same or similar information, be wary of trusting the validity of information.

A simple way to evaluate websites is to use a checklist (see next page). Once you've had enough practice finding and evaluating websites that fulfill your research goals, you won't need to use a checklist. You'll *automatically* find yourself checking the points mentioned to evaluate a site more rapidly. Won't that be great? The bottom line: Always evaluate any site you plan to use in your academic work, particularly the validity of the site. Don't skip this step to save time. You might be putting your college success in jeopardy. Try using the Website Evaluation Checklist on the following page. You can tear it out and make copies to use when you do Internet research.

QUICK TIP

Filling out a checklist sheet for each source you use makes it quick and easy to cite your sources on the Reference page of your written document.

Website Evaluation Checklist

Who sponsored the site?

Look at the domain at the end of the Web address for clues:

> .edu = educational institution such as a school, college, or university
>
> .gov = government agency
>
> .org = usually (but not always) a nonprofit organization or political organization
>
> .mil = U.S. military
>
> .com = commercial site, including company websites and personal Web pages

Who's the author? (especially important if it's a .com site)

- What qualifications does he or she have?
- Does the website include biographical information? contact information?
- It may be necessary to use other sources to check the author's credentials.

What is its purpose?

- Is it biased, or does it promote a particular viewpoint? *If so, make sure you balance it with opposing information.*
- Is it selling or promoting a product or service?

Is the information accurate?

- Does the website document or cite its sources?
- Is it someone's personal opinion and not backed up by facts?
- Are there grammatical errors or typos?

Is the information current?

- When was the site created or last updated?
- Are there broken links? If so, the website may not be up to date.

See also *Evaluating Web Pages: Techniques to Apply & Questions to Ask* available at: http://www.lib.berkeley.edu/TeachingLib/Guides/Internet/Evaluate.html

4. WHEN AND HOW TO CITE WEB SOURCES Plagiarism is using someone else's information, not giving that person the credit, and passing it off as your own work. This is illegal, and most colleges have a policy forbidding it. Students should cite a source if using any of the following:

- A direct quote from a writer or speaker
- A paraphrase from a writer or speaker
- The same sequence of ideas as a specific source

Since so much of the information in today's world comes from the Internet, below is a guide for citing from a website.

How to cite *an article* from a website in MLA style:

Author(s) of Internet article. "Title of source (article)." *Title of container* (website), other contributors (such as editor of website), publisher, publication date, location (URL or DOI).

Source: MLA Handbook, Eighth edition, 2016.

When you cite sources, make sure you are using the most up-to-date MLA or APA formats.

Writing Like a Reader

Remember that paraphrases, or restatements of someone's thoughts and ideas in your own words, require giving proper credit, just as direct quotations do. Since plagiarism can result in a failing grade or even expulsion from school, it's important to understand how a proper paraphrase might

appear. Simply changing a few words or changing the sequence of information does not result in a proper paraphrase. Consider the paragraph
below and the example paraphrases that follow:

> When I was a young boy in Omaha, we never had a key to our
> house. The door was never locked. If our mother ever went to the
> hospital, the neighbor women would cook, clean, wash, and take
> care of everything. Now we don't even know many of our
> neighbors, and our doors are deadbolted. Some leave their outside
> lights on all night and have security systems for protection.
>
> —FROM MEMOIRS OF JOSEPH (CHIC) MANCUSO

Example of an **improper paraphrase:**

In the past, some people in Omaha had no house keys because doors were
never locked. When mothers went to the hospital, neighbor women would
wash, clean, cook, and take care of things. Now neighbors aren't as
friendly, doors are locked with deadbolts, and security systems are used.

Example of a **proper paraphrase:**

In his memoirs, Joseph (Chic) Mancuso describes how neighborhood
safety and relationships have changed in his lifetime. Unlocked doors and
close, helpful neighbors have been replaced with deadbolt locks and limited neighborly connections.

Strategy Area C: Word Processing Basics— A Reference Guide

Readiness Quiz C

Choose **T** for true or **F** for false after reading each statement below.

1. _____ I know how to use a word processing standard toolbar.

2. _____ I know how to create a new document.

3. _____ I know how to edit a document.

4. _____ I know how to save a document.

5. _____ I know how to reopen a saved document.

6. _____ I know how to format a document.

If you answered **F** to any of the above statements, please refer
to the appropriate section of the reference guide on the pages that
follow.

C. Word Processing Basics—A Reference Guide

The purpose of this section is to give you a quick reference guide to creating documents. Most of the work you do in a college classroom will require completed computer documents (typed). Often, students have not received computer training, but have acquired skills by watching others. Some students have not had any experience in creating a document on the computer, but can surf the Web. Some students have no computer experience at all. This is a straightforward guide to working with Microsoft Word, a software program available on most computers in colleges across the country.

BASIC WORD PROCESSING REFERENCE GUIDE FOR MICROSOFT WORD

The Standard Toolbar

Function of Commonly Used Buttons

Creates a new blank document based on the default template

Opens or finds a file

Saves the active file with its current file name, location, and file format

Prints the active file - for more print options go to the File menu and select Print

Print preview - Shows how the document will look when you print it.

Spelling, grammar, and writing style checker

Cut - Removes the selection from the document and places it on the clipboard

Copy - Copies the selected item(s) to the clipboard

Paste - Places the content of the clipboard at the insertion point

Format painter - Copies the format from a selected object or text and applies to other objects or text

Undo - Reverses the last command, use pull-down menu to undo several steps

Redo - Reverses the action of the Undo button, use the pull-down menu to redo several steps

Displays the Tables and Borders toolbar

Inserts a table into the document, or make a table of selected text

Inserts an Excel spreadsheet into the Word document

Columns - Changes the number of columns in a document

Displays or hides the Drawing toolbar

Zoom - Enlarges or reduces the display of the active document

CREATING A DOCUMENT

1. Open Microsoft Word by clicking on the icon or locating it by pressing the Start key.
2. Begin to type your document.
   - Press the Enter key only to start a new paragraph.
   - Use the Backspace key or the Delete key to remove unwanted letters, words, or sentences.
3. As you type, save what you have done every 10 to 15 minutes.
4. If a word is underlined with a red or green wavy line, right-click on the word, and select from the list of suggested spellings or grammar corrections.
5. Use the Print Preview button to see what your document will look like once you have printed it.
6. If it looks the way you would like for it to look, save it before printing.
7. To print, click the Print button on the standard tool bar.
8. To close your document, click the File menu, and select the Close option, or click the X in top right corner of page.

EDITING A DOCUMENT

1. Highlight the text to be moved or copied.
2. Click the Cut button if you want to move the text to a different location *or*
3. Click the Copy button if you want to copy the text.
4. Click where you want to paste the text, and then click the Paste button.

SAVING A DOCUMENT

1. Click the Save button on the standard tool bar.
2. Select Local Disk (C:) to save on the hard drive.
3. To save to a flash drive:
   - Click the Save button.
   - Click the down arrow in the list box.
   - Click F drive to save to the flash drive.
   - Type the file name in the File Name list box.
   - Click Save at the lower right corner of the dialog box.

REOPENING A DOCUMENT

1. Open Microsoft Word.
2. Click the Open button on the standard tool bar.

3. Click the drop-down arrow to specify the drive [Local Disk (C) or Flash Drive (F)].
4. Double-click the file name from the list of files available.

FORMATTING A DOCUMENT

The Formatting Toolbar

| Normal ▾ | Arial ▾ | 12 ▾ | **B** | *I* | U | ≡ ≡ ≡ ≡ | ⋮≡ ⋮≡ ⋮≡ ⋮≡ | ☐ ▾ ⬟ ▾ A ▾ |

Function of Commonly Used Buttons

Normal ▾ — Selects the style to apply to paragraphs	Arial ▾ — Changes the font of the selected text
12 ▾ — Changes the size of selected text and numbers	**B** — Makes selected text and numbers bold
I — Makes selected text and numbers italic	U — Underlines selected text and numbers
≡ — Aligns to the left with a ragged right margin	≡ — Centers the selected text
≡ — Aligns to the right with a ragged left margin	≡ — Aligns the selected text to both the left and right margins
⋮≡ — Makes a numbered list or reverts back to normal	⋮≡ — Adds or removes bullets in a selected paragraph
⋮≡ — Decreases the indent to the previous tab stop	⋮≡ — Indents the selected paragraph to the next tab stop
☐ ▾ — Adds or removes a border around selected text or objects	⬟ ▾ — Marks text so that it is highlighted and stands out
A ▾ — Formats the selected text with the color you click	

1. Highlight the text to be formatted.
2. Change the style of the text by clicking the Bold **B**, Italic *I*, or Underline U button from the Formatting Toolbar.
3. Change the font type by selecting a font from the Font List Arial ▾ on the Formatting Toolbar.

4. Change the font size by selecting the size from the Font Size `12 ▾` list on the Formatting Toolbar.

5. Create a bulleted or numbered list by clicking the Bullets `☰` button or the Numbering `☷` button.

6. Create a border around the page by clicking the Format menu, borders and shading, page border, and then selecting the border you like.

7. Change the document's margins by clicking the File menu, page set-up, margin tab, and then adjust the margins.

8. Add a header or footer by clicking the View menu, header and footer, then type what will be shown in the area.

9. Double-space the document by clicking the Format menu, paragraph, line spacing, and then select Double from the drop-down list.

QUICK TIP

Remember . . . You can also use keyboard shortcuts such as:

- Ctrl + A (select All)
- Ctrl + C (Copy)
- Ctrl + V (Paste)
- Ctrl + P (Print)
- Ctrl + Z (Undo)
- Ctrl + S (Save file)
- Ctrl + X (Cut)

Chapter Summary

Searching the Internet: In order to search effectively on the Internet, it's important to be familiar with the term and concept of the World Wide Web, to understand four key factors involved in a search, and to know the basics of beginning a search.

- ***World Wide Web (WWW or W3):*** An interconnected, hypertext-based network that allows you to browse a variety of Internet resources organized by home pages.
- ***Four Key Components:*** Include use of a browser, a search engine, Web pages, and links.

• *Beginning a Search:* Begin by opening a search engine, determining the topic of the search, identifying key words for the search, typing the key words into the search box, and finally, analyzing the search results.

Evaluating Websites: Entails determining the purpose of the search and then analyzing sites for ease of use and validity of information.

• *Purpose of Search:* To save time and effort, set a research goal before beginning the search for information. Determine what type of site will best meet your goal.

• *Ease of Use:* Major factors include a site's design and its navigability. Skim the home page (and other pages) for eye appeal and ease of use. Determine if it's organized in a sensible way.

• *Validity of Information:* Determining the validity of the information on a website is the most important part of the evaluation process. Things to consider include the sponsor and author of the site, the dates of the information on the site and when it was last updated, the content itself, copyright issues, and whether or not other sites or sources corroborate the content of the site.

• *Citing Web Sources:* Cite sources if using direct quotes or paraphrasing, and when following the same sequence of ideas as the original source. Use the citation format required by your instructor.

Word Processing Basics: Consult the brief guide at the end of this chapter for basic information on using a standard toolbar, and for creating, editing, saving, reopening, and formatting documents.

Check Your Learning (Learning Outcomes)

Have you mastered the Learning Objectives (LOs) for Chapter 8? Place a check mark next to each LO that you're able to do.

PART A

_____ LO1—Conduct an Internet search using the World Wide Web

_____ LO2—Differentiate between the four key components of an Internet search

_____ LO3—Begin a purposeful Internet search

PART B

_____ LO1—Determine if a site meets the purpose of your search

_____ LO2—Evaluate a site's design and navigability (ease of use)

_____ LO3—Assess the validity of website information

_____ LO4—Correctly cite Web sources

PART C

_____ LO1—Review, as needed, some of the basic concepts of word processing using the reference guide in this section.

Go back and review the sections that cover any LO you didn't check.

Quick Connections—Chapter Eight

NEWS SOURCE CONNECTION

Using the Internet, find and skim three different news websites to compare and contrast the reports on a current event topic of your choice. Be sure to identify the websites used. You may report your results in paragraph format, or you may use a graphic organizer such as a comparison/contrast chart.

TEXTBOOK CONNECTION

Use a textbook from one of your other classes (or a sample chapter provided by your instructor). Select an interesting topic that is addressed in the text or sample chapter. Then use the Internet to search for, and list, websites that address the same topic. Check for corroboration of specific ideas between the sites and the text. Write a brief report on your findings, and be sure to include your list of sites.

NOVEL CONNECTION

Use the Internet to locate additional information on the author of a novel you're reading in your current reading class. Create a list of sites you found, and write a one-page summary of your findings.

WEB CONNECTION

Choose a topic from this course (or one of your other courses this term) to research on the Internet. Find at least five sites, and list them. Evaluate two of the five sites, using the evaluation checklist included in this chapter. Use a word processor to type a brief report on your findings.

Below are some other sites you could use instead of, or in addition to, the site listed earlier in this chapter:

http://www.lib.berkeley.edu/TeachingLib/Guides/Internet/Evaluate.html

http://www.library.cornell.edu/olinuris/ref/research/webeval.html

http://www.virtualchase.com/quality/

Credits

FM: Monkey Business Images/Shutterstock **p. 26,** Vrij, Aldert. Detecting Lies and Deceit: The Psychology of Lying and Implications for Professional Practice. Chichester: John Wiley & Sons, 2000; Olsen, D. E., Harris, J. C., Capps, M. H. & Ansley, N. (1997). Computerized polygraph scoring system. Journal of Forensic Sciences, 42, 61–70; William M. Oliver. *Community Oriented Policing 2e.* Upper Saddle River: Prentice Hall, 2001; Prentice Hall website, http://www.prenticehall.com; Thottam, Jyoti. Whose Plan Is Better? By Jyoti Thottam, Saturday, Sept. 04, 2004, Time Magazine; **p. 30,** Goldwater, Barry. 'Why Gun Control Laws Don't Work.' Reader's Digest Dec. 1975: 183–188; **p. 31,** Johnson, McNally, & Essay, *Essentials of Dental Radiography for Dental Assistants and Hygienists 7e.* Pearson Education Inc., 2003; McLaughlin, Susan, & Margolskee, Rorbert F (November–December 1994), The Sense of Taste American Scientist 82 (6), pp. 538–545; Erickson, DiLorenzo, & Woodbury, Classification of taste responses in brain stem: membership in fuzzy sets. Erickson RP, Di Lorenzo PM, Woodbury MA., Journal Neurophysiology. 1994 Jun;71(6):2139–50. **p. 32,** Whitford, Ben. "Keeping Her Promise to Our Kids" by *Newsweek*, October 3, 2005; **p. 66,** Kluger, Jeffrey. Lord of the Rings. Time , June 28, 2004; Benokraitis, Nijole V., Marriages and Families, 5th Ed., ©2005. Reprinted and Electronically reproduced by permission of Pearson Education, Inc., New York, NY. **p. 74,** Yann Martel. *Life of Pi.* New York: Harcourt Inc., 2001. **p. 76,** Dave Pelzer. A Child Called "IT." Deerfield Beach: Health Communications Inc., 1995; **p. 77,** Berliner, Michael, "The Christopher Columbus Controversy: Western Civilization vs. Primitivism," October 14, 1999. Appearing in CAPITALISM MAGAZINE. Copyright by the Ayn Rand Institute. **p. 80,** The Scarlet Letter by Nathaniel Hawthorne, 1850; Ann Rand Web site, www.aynrand.org; Nguyen, Vienney and Blaine Lilly, Carlos Castro. Journal of Biomechanics, The exoskeletal structure and tensile loading behavior of an ant neck joint, Vienny Nguyen, Blaine Lilly, Carlos Castro, January 22, 2014 Volume 47, Issue 2, Pages 497–504; **p. 82,** "Let's Look for New Candidates," *Omaha World Herald*, April 16, 2016; **p. 88,** Elie Wiesel. *Night.* New York: Random House, Inc., 1960; **p. 95,** Thomas, Lewis. The Attic of the Brain, essay from Late Night Thoughts on Listening to Mahler's Ninth Symphony by Lewis Thomas, 1995, Penguin; **p. 95, 96, 97,** Albom, Mitch. Tuesdays with Morrie : An Old Man, A Young Man and Life's Greatest Lesson, by Mitch Albom, Doubleday, U.S.A. (1997); **p. 98,** Towne, Charles, Hanson. Of One Self-Slain from A World of Windows: And Other Poems By Charles Hanson Towne, 1919, George H. Doran company; **p. 99,** Ford, J., '20/20 Hindsight', in Sheena Gillespie and Robert Singleton, eds., Across Cultures, Boston: 1996, Allyn and Bacon; **p. 100,** Voskamp, Ann. One Thousand Gifts: A Dare to Live Fully Right Where You Are, by Ann Voskamp, Zondervan 2011; **p. 101,** Kirkpatrick, Betty. Cliches: Over 1500 Phrases Explored and Explained, by Betty Kirkpatrick, Bloomsbury Publishing Plc, 1996; **p. 103,** De Vries, Peter. Let Me Count the Ways, 1965, Little Brown & Company, Boston, p. 307; **p. 111,** Mancuso, Joseph (Chic), THINGS I REMEMBER GROWING UP", From the Memoirs of Joseph (Chic) Mancuso; **p. 120,** Elder, Linda, "What is Critical Thinking?" Foundation for

Index

Italics indicate illustrations, tables, or sidebars.